COOK smart

CUPCAKES

igloobooks

igloobooks

Published in 2015
by Igloo Books Ltd
Cottage Farm
Sywell
NN6 0BJ
www.igloobooks.com

Food photography and recipe development: PhotoCuisine UK
Front and back cover images © PhotoCuisine UK

LEO002 0115
2 4 6 8 10 9 7 5 3 1
ISBN 978-1-78440-153-5

Printed and manufactured in China

Contents

Classic
Cupcakes

Cherry swirl cupcakes

Preparation time
45 minutes

Cooking time
18 minutes

Makes 12

Ingredients

110 g / 4 oz / 1 cup self-raising flour, sifted

110 g / 4 oz / ½ cup caster (superfine) sugar

110 g / 4 oz / ½ cup butter, softened

2 large eggs

1 tsp almond extract

100 g / 3 ½ oz / ½ cup glacé cherries, quartered

To decorate:

110 g / 4 oz / ½ cup butter, softened

225 g / 8 oz / 2 cups icing (confectioners') sugar, plus extra for dusting

1 tbsp cherry syrup

a few drops of pink food dye

12 fresh cherries with stems

Method

1. Preheat the oven to 190°C (170°C fan) / 375F / gas 5 and line a 12-hole cupcake tin with paper cases.

2. Combine the flour, sugar, butter, eggs and almond extract in a bowl and whisk together for 2 minutes or until smooth, then fold in the glacé cherries.

3. Divide the mixture between the cake cases, then transfer the tin to the oven and bake for 18 minutes. Test with a wooden toothpick; if it comes out clean, the cakes are done. Transfer the cakes to a wire rack and leave to cool completely.

4. To make the buttercream, beat the butter until smooth then beat in the icing sugar.

5. Spoon half of the buttercream down one side of a piping bag fitted with a large star nozzle. Beat the cherry syrup and a few drops of food dye into the rest of the buttercream and spoon it into the other side of the bag. Pipe a spiral of buttercream onto each cake and top each one with a fresh cherry.

Smart tip

Start the buttercream
spiral from the outside
of the cake and work
towards the centre to
create a classic swirl.

Smart tip

Add the lemon juice a few drops at a time as the icing can go runny very quickly.

Lemon and poppy seed cupcakes

Preparation time
30 minutes

Cooking time
18 minutes

Makes 12

Ingredients

110 g / 4 oz / 1 cup
   self-raising flour, sifted
110 g / 4 oz / ½ cup caster
   (superfine) sugar
110 g / 4 oz / ½ cup butter,
   softened
2 large eggs
2 tbsp poppy seeds
1 lemon, zest finely grated

To decorate:
200 g / 7 oz / 2 cups icing
   (confectioners') sugar, plus
   extra for dusting
1 lemon, juiced

Method

1. Preheat the oven to 190°C (170°C fan) / 375F / gas 5 and line a 12-hole cupcake tin with paper cases.

2. Combine the flour, sugar, butter, eggs, poppy seeds and lemon zest in a bowl and whisk together for 2 minutes or until smooth.

3. Divide the mixture between the cases, then transfer the tin to the oven and bake for 18 minutes or until a skewer inserted in the centre of a cake comes out clean. Transfer the cakes to a wire rack and leave to cool completely.

4. Sieve the icing sugar into a bowl and add just enough lemon juice to make a thick, pourable icing.

5. Drizzle the icing over the cakes and dust with icing sugar.

Raspberry and white chocolate cupcakes

Preparation time
45 minutes

Cooking time
18 minutes

Makes 12

Ingredients

110 g / 4 oz / 1 cup self-raising flour, sifted
110 g / 4 oz / ½ cup caster (superfine) sugar
110 g / 4 oz / ½ cup butter, softened
2 large eggs
1 tsp vanilla extract
16 raspberries, quartered
4 tbsp white chocolate, finely chopped

To decorate:

110 g / 4 oz / ½ cup butter, softened
225 g / 8 oz / 2 cups icing (confectioners') sugar, plus extra for dusting
4 tbsp white chocolate, finely chopped
12 raspberries

Method

1. Preheat the oven to 190°C (170°C fan) / 375F / gas 5 and line a 12-hole cupcake tin with paper cases.

2. Combine the flour, sugar, butter, eggs and vanilla extract in a bowl and whisk together for 2 minutes or until smooth, then fold in the raspberries and white chocolate.

3. Divide the mixture between the cake cases, then transfer the tin to the oven and bake for 18 minutes. Test with a wooden toothpick; if it comes out clean, the cakes are done. Transfer the cakes to a wire rack and leave to cool completely.

4. To make the buttercream, beat the butter until smooth then beat in the icing sugar. Spoon the mixture into a piping bag fitted with a large star nozzle and pipe a swirl on top of each cake. Sprinkle the centre of each cake with chopped white chocolate and top with the raspberries.

Smart tip
Serve these cakes
straight away to enjoy
the cream at its best.

Blueberry pie cupcakes

Preparation time
45 minutes

Cooking time
18 minutes

Makes 12

Ingredients

110 g / 4 oz / 1 cup self-raising
   flour, sifted
110 g / 4 oz / ½ cup caster
   (superfine) sugar
110 g / 4 oz / ½ cup butter,
   softened
2 large eggs
1 tsp vanilla extract
75 g / 2 ½ oz / ½ cup
   blueberries

To decorate:
300 ml / 10 ½ fl. oz / 1 ¼ cups
   double (heavy) cream
36 blueberries

Method

1. Preheat the oven to 190°C (170°C fan) / 375F / gas 5 and line
   a 12-hole cupcake tin with paper cases.

2. Combine the flour, sugar, butter, eggs and vanilla extract in a
   bowl and whisk together for 2 minutes or until smooth, then
   fold in the blueberries.

3. Divide the mixture between the cake cases, then transfer the
   tin to the oven and bake for 18 minutes. Test with a wooden
   toothpick; if it comes out clean, the cakes are done. Transfer
   the cakes to a wire rack and leave to cool completely.

4. Whip the cream until it holds its shape, then spoon it into a
   piping bag fitted with a large star nozzle. Pipe the cream onto
   the cakes and top each one with three blueberries.

Chocolate espresso cupcakes

Preparation time
35 minutes

Cooking time
18 minutes

Makes 12

Ingredients

110 g / 4 oz / 1 cup
self-raising flour, sifted
110 g / 4 oz / ½ cup caster
(superfine) sugar
110 g / 4 oz / ½ cup butter,
softened
2 large eggs
2 tbsp unsweetened cocoa
powder
1 tbsp instant espresso
powder

To decorate:
100 g / 3 ½ oz / ½ cup butter,
softened
200 g / 7 oz / 2 cups icing
(confectioners') sugar
2 tsp instant espresso powder
36 chocolate-covered coffee
beans

Method

1. Preheat the oven to 190°C (170°C fan) / 375F / gas 5 and line a 12-hole cupcake tin with paper cases.

2. Combine the flour, sugar, butter, eggs, cocoa and espresso powder in a bowl and whisk together for 2 minutes or until smooth.

3. Divide the mixture between the cases, then transfer the tin to the oven and bake for 18 minutes. Test with a wooden toothpick; if it comes out clean, the cakes are done. Transfer the cakes to a wire rack and leave to cool completely.

4. Beat the butter until smooth, then gradually whisk in the icing sugar and espresso powder.

5. Spoon the icing into a piping bag fitted with a large star nozzle and pipe a big swirl on top of the cakes. Finish each cake with three chocolate-covered coffee beans.

Smart tip
Serve straight away
for the raspberries to
be at their best.

Raspberry swirl cupcakes

Preparation time
45 minutes

Cooking time
18 minutes

Makes 12

Ingredients

110 g / 4 oz / 1 cup self-raising
  flour, sifted
110 g / 4 oz / ½ cup caster
  (superfine) sugar
110 g / 4 oz / ½ cup butter,
  softened
2 large eggs
1 tsp vanilla extract

To decorate:

110 g / 4 oz / ½ cup butter,
  softened
225 g / 8 oz / 2 cups icing
  (confectioners') sugar, plus
  extra for dusting
4 tbsp raspberry syrup
12 raspberries
12 small mint sprigs
icing (confectioners') sugar
  to dust

Method

1. Preheat the oven to 190°C (170°C fan) / 375F / gas 5 and line a 12-hole cupcake tin with paper cases.

2. Combine the flour, sugar, butter, eggs and vanilla extract in a bowl and whisk together for 2 minutes or until smooth.

3. Divide the mixture between the cake cases, then transfer the tin to the oven and bake for 18 minutes. Test with a wooden toothpick; if it comes out clean, the cakes are done. Transfer the cakes to a wire rack and leave to cool completely.

4. To make the buttercream, beat the butter until smooth, then beat in the icing sugar and half of the raspberry syrup.

5. Drizzle the rest of the syrup around the inside of a piping bag fitted with a large star nozzle then fill it with the buttercream. Pipe a swirl on top of each cake and top with the raspberries, mint leaves and icing sugar.

Chocolate orange cupcakes

Preparation time
1 hour

Cooking time
18 minutes

Makes 12

Ingredients

110 g / 4 oz / 1 cup self-raising
  flour, sifted
2 tbsp cocoa powder
110 g / 4 oz / ½ cup caster
  (superfine) sugar
110 g / 4 oz / ½ cup butter,
  softened
2 large eggs
1 orange, zest finely grated
50 g / 1 ¾ oz / ⅓ cup orange
  chocolate, chopped

To decorate:
110 g / 4 oz / ½ cup butter,
  softened
225 g / 8 oz / 2 cups icing
  (confectioners') sugar, plus
  extra for dusting
1 orange, juiced and zest
  finely grated
cocoa powder for dusting
100 g / 3 ½ oz / ½ cup ready-
  to-roll fondant icing
orange and green food dye

Method

1. Preheat the oven to 190°C (170°C fan) / 375F / gas 5 and line
   a 12-hole cupcake tin with paper cases.

2. Combine the flour, cocoa powder, sugar, butter, eggs and
   orange zest in a bowl and whisk together for 2 minutes or
   until smooth, then fold in the orange chocolate.

3. Divide the mixture between the cake cases, then transfer the
   tin to the oven and bake for 18 minutes. Test with a wooden
   toothpick; if it comes out clean, the cakes are done. Transfer
   the cakes to a wire rack and leave to cool completely.

4. To make the buttercream, beat the butter until smooth, then
   beat in the icing sugar, orange zest and 1 tbsp of the juice.
   Spoon the mixture into a piping bag fitted with a large plain
   nozzle and pipe a swirl on top of each cake. Dust with a little
   cocoa powder.

5. Dye three quarters of the fondant orange and shape balls
   to make into the oranges. Turn the rest green and make the
   leaves, attaching with a dab of water. Sit a fondant orange on
   top of each cake.

Smart tip

Use a tea strainer to sprinkle the cocoa powder for even coverage.

Smart tip
Use the lavender essence sparingly as it has a very strong taste.

Iced lavender cupcakes

Preparation time
30 minutes

Cooking time
18 minutes

Makes 12

Ingredients

110 g / 4 oz / 1 cup self-raising
    flour, sifted
110 g / 4 oz / ½ cup caster
    (superfine) sugar
110 g / 4 oz / ½ cup butter,
    softened
2 large eggs
a few drops of culinary
    lavender essence

To decorate:
300 g / 10 ½ oz / 3 cups icing
    (confectioners') sugar, plus
    extra for dusting
1 lemon, juiced
a few drops of purple food
    dye
12 lavender sprigs

Method

1. Preheat the oven to 190°C (170°C fan) / 375F / gas 5 and line
   a 12-hole cupcake tin with paper cases.

2. Combine the flour, sugar, butter, eggs and lavender essence
   in a bowl and whisk together for 2 minutes or until smooth.

3. Divide the mixture between the cases, then transfer the tin to
   the oven and bake for 18 minutes or until a skewer inserted
   comes out clean. Transfer the cakes to a wire rack and leave to
   cool completely.

4. Sieve the icing sugar into a bowl and add just enough
   lemon juice to make a thick, pourable icing. Add a few
   drops of purple food dye to the icing until it turns a very
   pale shade of lavender.

5. Spoon a thick layer of icing onto the cakes, spreading it out
   with the back of the spoon. Top each cake with a sprig of
   lavender.

Milk chocolate swirl cupcakes

Preparation time
45 minutes

Cooking time
18 minutes

Makes 12

Ingredients

110 g / 4 oz / 1 cup self-raising
  flour, sifted
110 g / 4 oz / ½ cup caster
  (superfine) sugar
110 g / 4 oz / ½ cup butter,
  softened
2 large eggs
1 tsp vanilla extract
50 g / 1 ¾ oz / ⅓ cup milk
  chocolate, chopped

To decorate:

110 g / 4 oz / ½ cup butter,
  softened
225 g / 8 oz / 2 cups icing
  (confectioners') sugar, plus
  extra for dusting
2 tbsp cocoa powder
12 pieces of milk chocolate

Method

1. Preheat the oven to 190°C (170°C fan) / 375F / gas 5 and line a 12-hole cupcake tin with paper cases.

2. Combine the flour, sugar, butter, eggs and vanilla extract in a bowl and whisk together for 2 minutes or until smooth, then fold in the chocolate.

3. Divide the mixture between the cake cases, then transfer the tin to the oven and bake for 18 minutes. Test with a wooden toothpick; if it comes out clean, the cakes are done. Transfer the cakes to a wire rack and leave to cool completely.

4. To make the buttercream, beat the butter until smooth, then beat in the icing sugar and cocoa powder. Spoon the mixture into a piping bag fitted with a large star nozzle and pipe a swirl on top of each cake. Top each one with a piece of chocolate.

Smart tip

If the buttercream is too stiff, add a drop of milk and whisk until smooth.

Smart tip

Use a tea strainer to get a light, even sprinkle of cocoa powder.

Café latte cupcakes

Preparation time
40 minutes

Cooking time
18 minutes

Makes 12

Ingredients

110 g / 4 oz / 1 cup self-raising
  flour, sifted
110 g / 4 oz / ½ cup caster
  (superfine) sugar
110 g / 4 oz / ½ cup butter,
  softened
2 large eggs
1 tbsp instant espresso
  powder

To decorate:
100 g / 3 ½ oz / ½ cup butter,
  softened
200 g / 7 oz / 2 cups icing
  (confectioners') sugar
1 tsp instant espresso powder
12 chocolate-covered coffee
  beans
cocoa powder for sprinkling

Method

1. Preheat the oven to 190°C (170°C fan) / 375F / gas 5 and line
   a 12-hole cupcake tin with paper cases.
2. Combine the flour, sugar, butter, eggs and espresso powder
   in a bowl and whisk together for 2 minutes or until smooth.
3. Divide the mixture between the cases, then transfer the tin
   to the oven and bake for 18 minutes. Test with a wooden
   toothpick; if it comes out clean, the cakes are done. Transfer
   the cakes to a wire rack and leave to cool completely.
4. To decorate the cakes, beat the butter until smooth then
   gradually whisk in the icing sugar and espresso powder.
5. Spoon the icing into a piping bag fitted with a large star
   nozzle and pipe a swirl onto each cake. Top the cakes with
   a coffee bean and a sprinkle of cocoa powder.

Black cherry cream cupcakes

Preparation time
40 minutes

Cooking time
18 minutes

Makes 12

Ingredients

110 g / 4 oz / 1 cup self-raising flour, sifted
110 g / 4 oz / ½ cup caster (superfine) sugar
110 g / 4 oz / ½ cup butter, softened
2 large eggs
1 tsp almond extract

To decorate:
300 ml / 10 ½ fl. oz / 1 ¼ cups double (heavy) cream
110 g / 4 oz / ½ cup black cherry jam (jelly)

Method

1. Preheat the oven to 190°C (170°C fan) / 375F / gas 5 and line a 12-hole cupcake tin with paper cases.

2. Combine the flour, sugar, butter, eggs and almond extract in a bowl and whisk together for 2 minutes or until smooth.

3. Divide the mixture between the cake cases, then transfer the tin to the oven and bake for 18 minutes. Test with a wooden toothpick; if it comes out clean, the cakes are done. Transfer the cakes to a wire rack and leave to cool completely.

4. Whip the cream until it holds its shape, then spoon it into a piping bag fitted with a large star nozzle.

5. Pipe a ring on top of the cake and fill with cherry jam.

Smart tip

Using almond extract in
the cakes brings out the
cherry taste of the jam.

Smart tip

Leave the chocolate to cool a little after melting so that it doesn't melt the buttercream.

Chocolate drizzle cupcakes

Preparation time
40 minutes

Cooking time
18 minutes

Makes 12

Ingredients

110 g / 4 oz / 1 cup self-raising
  flour, sifted
110 g / 4 oz / ½ cup caster
  (superfine) sugar
110 g / 4 oz / ½ cup butter,
  softened
2 large eggs
2 tbsp unsweetened cocoa
  powder

To decorate:
100 g / 3 ½ oz / ½ cup butter,
  softened
200 g / 7 oz / 2 cups icing
  (confectioners') sugar
1 tsp vanilla extract
50 g / 1 ¾ oz / ⅓ cup milk
  chocolate

Method

1. Preheat the oven to 190°C (170°C fan) / 375F / gas 5 and line
   a 12-hole cupcake tin with paper cases.
2. Combine the flour, sugar, butter, eggs and cocoa powder in a
   bowl and whisk together for 2 minutes or until smooth.
3. Divide the mixture between the cases, then transfer the tin
   to the oven and bake for 18 minutes. Test with a wooden
   toothpick; if it comes out clean, the cakes are done. Transfer
   the cakes to a wire rack and leave to cool completely.
4. Beat the butter until smooth, then gradually whisk in the icing
   sugar and vanilla extract.
5. Spoon the buttercream into a piping bag fitted with a large
   star nozzle and pipe it onto the cakes.
6. Melt the chocolate in a microwave or bain-marie, then use a
   teaspoon to drizzle it over the cakes.

Butterscotch cupcakes

Preparation time
45 minutes

Cooking time
18 minutes

Makes 12

Ingredients

110 g / 4 oz / 1 cup self-raising
  flour, sifted
110 g / 4 oz / ½ cup caster
  (superfine) sugar
110 g / 4 oz / ½ cup butter,
  softened
2 large eggs
2 tbsp unsweetened cocoa
  powder
3 tbsp butterscotch pieces

To decorate:
100 ml / 3 ½ fl. oz / ½ cup
  butterscotch sauce
300 ml / 10 ½ fl. oz / 1 ¼ cups
  double (heavy) cream
2 tbsp milk chocolate, grated

Method

1. Preheat the oven to 190°C (170°C fan) / 375F / gas 5 and line a 12-hole cupcake tin with paper cases.

2. Combine the flour, sugar, butter, eggs and cocoa in a bowl and whisk together for 2 minutes or until smooth, then fold in the butterscotch pieces.

3. Divide the mixture between the cases, then transfer the tin to the oven and bake for 18 minutes. Test with a wooden toothpick; if it comes out clean, the cakes are done. Transfer the cakes to a wire rack and leave to cool completely.

4. Reserve 4 tbsp of the butterscotch sauce, then put the rest in a bowl with the cream and whip until it holds its shape. Spoon the cream into a piping bag fitted with a large star nozzle and pipe a swirl on top of each cake.

5. Top with the reserved butterscotch sauce and sprinkle with grated chocolate.

Smart tip

If you can't find
butterscotch pieces,
put a few butterscotch
sweets in a bag and
bash with a rolling pin.

Smart tip
Fresh ripe peach slices
can also be used when
in season.

Peach Melba cupcakes

Preparation time
45 minutes

Cooking time
18 minutes

Makes 12

Ingredients

110 g / 4 oz / 1 cup self-raising
  flour, sifted
110 g / 4 oz / ½ cup caster
  (superfine) sugar
110 g / 4 oz / ½ cup butter,
  softened
2 large eggs
1 tsp almond extract
3 tbsp freeze-dried raspberry
  pieces

To decorate:
300 ml / 10 ½ fl. oz / 1 ¼ cups
  double (heavy) cream
12 raspberries
12 canned peach slices
2 tbsp ground almonds

Method

1. Preheat the oven to 190°C (170°C fan) / 375F / gas 5 and line
   a 12-hole cupcake tin with paper cases.

2. Combine the flour, sugar, butter, eggs and almond extract in
   a bowl and whisk together for 2 minutes or until smooth, then
   fold in the raspberry pieces.

3. Divide the mixture between the cake cases, then transfer the
   tin to the oven and bake for 18 minutes. Test with a wooden
   toothpick; if it comes out clean, the cakes are done. Transfer
   the cakes to a wire rack and leave to cool completely.

4. Whip the cream until it holds its shape, then spoon it into a
   piping bag fitted with a large plain nozzle. Pipe the cream
   onto the cakes and top each one with a raspberry, a peach
   slice and a sprinkle of ground almonds.

Chocolate walnut cupcakes

Preparation time
45 minutes

Cooking time
18 minutes

Makes 12

Ingredients

110 g / 4 oz / 1 cup self-raising
    flour, sifted
2 tbsp cocoa powder
110 g / 4 oz / ½ cup caster
    (superfine) sugar
110 g / 4 oz / ½ cup butter,
    softened
2 large eggs
75 g / 1 ¾ oz / ⅔ cup walnuts,
    chopped

To decorate:
110 g / 4 oz / ½ cup butter,
    softened
225 g / 8 oz / 2 cups icing
    (confectioners') sugar, plus
    extra for dusting
1 tbsp walnut oil
1 tbsp cocoa powder
50 g / 1 ¾ oz / ½ cup walnuts,
    chopped

Method

1. Preheat the oven to 190°C (170°C fan) / 375F / gas 5 and line a 12-hole cupcake tin with paper cases.

2. Combine the flour, cocoa, sugar, butter and eggs in a bowl and whisk together for 2 minutes or until smooth, then fold in the walnuts.

3. Divide the mixture between the cake cases then transfer the tin to the oven and bake for 18 minutes. Test with a wooden toothpick; if it comes out clean, the cakes are done. Transfer the cakes to a wire rack and leave to cool completely.

4. To make the buttercream, beat the butter until smooth then beat in the icing sugar, walnut oil and cocoa powder. Spoon the mixture into a piping bag fitted with a large star nozzle and pipe a large rosette on top of each cake. Top with chopped walnuts.

Smart tip

Hold the piping bag just above the cake and squeeze to create the rosette.

Smart tip

Try soaking the raisins in rum for half an hour before using, for a stronger taste.

Rum and raisin cupcakes

Preparation time
45 minutes

Cooking time
18 minutes

Makes 12

Ingredients

110 g / 4 oz / 1 cup self-raising
   flour, sifted
110 g / 4 oz / ½ cup caster
   (superfine) sugar
110 g / 4 oz / ½ cup butter,
   softened
2 large eggs
1 tsp vanilla extract
75 g / 2 ½ oz / ⅓ cup raisins
3 tbsp white rum

To decorate:
110 g / 4 oz / ½ cup butter,
   softened
225 g / 8 oz / 2 cups icing
   (confectioners') sugar, plus
   extra for dusting
1 tbsp white rum
36 raisins

Method

1. Preheat the oven to 190°C (170°C fan) / 375F / gas 5 and line a 12-hole cupcake tin with paper cases.

2. Combine the flour, sugar, butter, eggs and vanilla extract in a bowl and whisk together for 2 minutes or until smooth, then fold in the raisins.

3. Divide the mixture between the cake cases, then transfer the tin to the oven and bake for 18 minutes. Test with a wooden toothpick; if it comes out clean, the cakes are done. Transfer the cakes to a wire rack, drizzle with rum and leave to cool completely.

4. To make the buttercream, beat the butter until smooth then beat in the icing sugar and rum.

5. Spoon the buttercream into a piping bag, fitted with a large star nozzle, then pipe a swirl onto each cake. Top each cake with three raisins to finish.

Chocolate butterfly cakes

Preparation time
45 minutes

Cooking time
10-15 minutes

Makes 12

Ingredients

110 g / 4 oz / 1 cup self-raising
   flour, sifted
110 g / 4 oz / ½ cup caster
   (superfine) sugar
110 g / 4 oz / ½ cup butter,
   softened
2 large eggs
1 tsp vanilla extract
2 tbsp unsweetened cocoa
   powder

To decorate:

110 g / 4 oz / ½ cup butter,
   softened
225 g / 8 oz / 2 cups icing
   (confectioners') sugar, plus
   extra for dusting
2 tbsp unsweetened cocoa
   powder
2 tbsp milk

Method

1. Preheat the oven to 190°C (170°C fan) / 375F / gas 5 and line
   a 12-hole cupcake tin with paper cases.

2. Combine the flour, sugar, butter, eggs, vanilla extract
   and cocoa in a bowl and whisk together for 2 minutes or
   until smooth.

3. Divide the mixture between the cake cases, then transfer
   the tin to the oven and bake for 10–15 minutes. Test with a
   wooden toothpick; if it comes out clean, the cakes are done.
   Transfer the cakes to a wire rack and leave to cool completely.

4. To make the buttercream, beat the butter until smooth then
   beat in the icing sugar and cocoa. Use a whisk to incorporate
   the milk, then whisk for 2 minutes or until well whipped.

5. Spoon the icing into a piping bag fitted with a large star
   nozzle. Using a sharp knife, cut a shallow cone out of the
   centre of each cake and reserve.

6. Pipe a swirl of buttercream into the centre of each cake.
   Take the reserved cake pieces and cut each one in half to
   make the butterfly wings.

Smart tip

The buttercream can be made a day in advance and stored in an airtight container in the fridge.

Smart tip

Taste the buttercream and add a little more mint syrup if needed.

Chocolate mint cupcakes

Preparation time
45 minutes

Cooking time
18 minutes

Makes 12

Ingredients

110 g / 4 oz / 1 cup self-raising
   flour, sifted
2 tbsp cocoa powder
110 g / 4 oz / ½ cup caster
   (superfine) sugar
110 g / 4 oz / ½ cup butter,
   softened
2 large eggs
1 tbsp peppermint syrup

To decorate:

110 g / 4 oz / ½ cup butter,
   softened
225 g / 8 oz / 2 cups icing
   (confectioners') sugar, plus
   extra for dusting
2 tbsp cocoa powder
1 tbsp peppermint syrup
150 ml / 5 ½ fl. oz / ⅔ cup
   double (heavy) cream
12 pieces mint chocolate
12 mint sprigs

Method

1. Preheat the oven to 190°C (170°C fan) / 375F / gas 5 and
   line a 12-hole cupcake tin with paper cases.

2. Combine the flour, cocoa, sugar, butter, eggs and
   peppermint syrup in a bowl and whisk together for
   2 minutes or until smooth.

3. Divide the mixture between the cake cases, then transfer the
   tin to the oven and bake for 18 minutes. Test with a wooden
   toothpick; if it comes out clean, the cakes are done. Transfer
   the cakes to a wire rack and leave to cool completely.

4. To make the buttercream, beat the butter until smooth then
   beat in the icing sugar, cocoa powder and mint syrup.

5. Spoon the mixture into a piping bag fitted with a large star
   nozzle and pipe a swirl on top of each cake.

6. Whip the cream until it holds its shape and pipe a rosette on
   top of the buttercream. Garnish with chocolate pieces and
   mint sprigs.

Carrot cream cheese cupcakes

Preparation time
1 hour

Cooking time
18 minutes

Makes 12

Ingredients

175 g / 6 oz / 1 cup soft light brown sugar
2 large eggs
150 ml / 5 fl. oz / ⅔ cup sunflower oil
175 g / 6 oz / 1 ¼ cups plain (all-purpose) flour
2 tsp baking powder
1 tsp ground ginger
1 orange, zest finely grated
200 g / 7 oz / 1 ⅔ cups carrots, peeled and coarsely grated

To decorate:
110 g / 4 oz / ½ cup cream cheese
55 g / 2 oz / ¼ cup butter, softened
110 g / 4 oz / 1 cup icing (confectioners') sugar
1 tbsp orange juice
150 g / 5 ½ oz / ¾ cup ready-to-roll fondant icing
orange and green food dye

Method

1. Preheat the oven to 190°C (170°C fan) / 375F / gas 5 and line a 12-hole cupcake tin with paper cases.

2. Whisk the sugar, eggs and oil together for 3 minutes. Fold in the flour, baking powder and ground ginger, followed by the orange zest and grated carrots.

3. Divide the mixture between the paper cases, then transfer the tin to the oven and bake for 18 minutes. Test with a wooden toothpick; if it comes out clean, the cakes are done. Transfer the cakes to a wire rack and leave to cool completely.

4. Beat the cream cheese and butter together until light and fluffy, then beat in the icing sugar a quarter at a time. Add the orange juice, then whip the mixture for 2 minutes or until smooth and light.

5. Spoon the icing into a piping bag fitted with a star nozzle and pipe a rosette onto each cake.

6. Dye two thirds of the fondant orange and shape into the carrots. Dye the rest green and make the tops, attaching with a dab of water. Plant a fondant carrot into the top of each cake.

Smart tip

Un-iced, these cakes keep well in an airtight container, but the frosting should be made and eaten on the same day.

Lemon meringue cupcakes

Preparation time
55 minutes

Cooking time
23 minutes

Makes 12

Ingredients

110 g / 4 oz / 1 cup self-raising flour, sifted

110 g / 4 oz / ½ cup caster (superfine) sugar

110 g / 4 oz / ½ cup butter, softened

1 lemon, zest finely grated

2 large eggs

To decorate:

4 large egg whites

110 g / 4 oz / ½ cup caster (superfine) sugar

100 ml / 3 ½ fl. oz / ½ cup lemon curd

Method

1. Preheat the oven to 190°C (170°C fan) / 375F / gas 5 and line a 12-hole cupcake tin with paper cases.

2. Whisk the cake ingredients together until smooth, then divide between the paper cases.

3. Bake for 18 minutes or until a skewer inserted in the centre of a cake comes out clean.

4. Whisk the egg whites until stiff, then gradually add the sugar and whisk until the mixture is thick and shiny. Spoon the meringue into a piping bag fitted with a large star nozzle.

5. Spoon some lemon curd onto each cake, then pipe a swirl of meringue on top.

6. Return the cakes to the oven and bake for a further 5 minutes or until golden brown.

Sweet Cupcakes

Blackcurrant cream cupcakes

Preparation time
45 minutes

Cooking time
18 minutes

Makes 12

Ingredients

110 g / 4 oz / 1 cup self-raising
   flour, sifted
110 g / 4 oz / ½ cup caster
   (superfine) sugar
110 g / 4 oz / ½ cup butter,
   softened
2 large eggs
1 tsp vanilla extract

To decorate:
300 ml / 10 ½ fl. oz / 1 ¼ cups
   double (heavy) cream
110 g / 4 oz / ½ cup
   blackcurrant jam (jelly)
icing (confectioners') sugar for
   dusting.

Method

1. Preheat the oven to 190°C (170°C fan) / 375F / gas 5 and line
   a 12-hole cupcake tin with paper cases.

2. Combine the flour, sugar, butter, eggs and vanilla extract in a
   bowl and whisk together for 2 minutes or until smooth.

3. Divide the mixture between the cake cases, then transfer the
   tin to the oven and bake for 18 minutes. Test with a wooden
   toothpick; if it comes out clean, the cakes are done. Transfer
   the cakes to a wire rack and leave to cool completely.

4. To decorate the cakes, whip the cream until it holds its shape
   then spoon it into a piping bag fitted with a large star nozzle.

5. Using a sharp knife, cut a shallow cone out of the centre of
   each cake and reserve.

6. Add a spoonful of jam to the centre of each cake, then pipe
   a little cream on top. Add the reserved cake cones and dust
   with icing sugar.

Smart tip

Use the best quality blackcurrant jam you can find.

Vanilla sprinkle cupcakes

Preparation time
45 minutes

Cooking time
18 minutes

Makes 12

Ingredients

110 g / 4 oz / 1 cup self-raising
   flour, sifted
110 g / 4 oz / ½ cup caster
   (superfine) sugar
110 g / 4 oz / ½ cup butter,
   softened
2 large eggs
1 tsp vanilla extract

To decorate:

110 g / 4 oz / ½ cup butter,
   softened
225 g / 8 oz / 2 cups icing
   (confectioners') sugar, plus
   extra for dusting
1 tsp vanilla extract
2 tbsp hundreds and
   thousands

Method

1. Preheat the oven to 190°C (170°C fan) / 375F / gas 5 and line
   a 12-hole cupcake tin with paper cases.

2. Combine the flour, sugar, butter, eggs and vanilla extract in a
   bowl and whisk together for 2 minutes or until smooth.

3. Divide the mixture between the cake cases, then transfer the
   tin to the oven and bake for 18 minutes. Test with a wooden
   toothpick; if it comes out clean, the cakes are done. Transfer
   the cakes to a wire rack and leave to cool completely.

4. To make the buttercream, beat the butter until smooth then
   beat in the icing sugar and vanilla extract.

5. Spoon the buttercream into a piping bag fitted with a large
   star nozzle and pipe a swirl onto each cake, then sprinkle with
   hundreds and thousands.

Orange crème cupcakes

Preparation time
40 minutes

Cooking time
18 minutes

Makes 12

Ingredients

110 g / 4 oz / 1 cup self-raising
flour, sifted
110 g / 4 oz / ½ cup caster
(superfine) sugar
110 g / 4 oz / ½ cup butter,
softened
2 large eggs
1 orange, zest finely grated

To decorate:
350 g / 12 oz / 1 ½ cups crème
fraiche
3 tbsp icing (confectioners')
sugar
1 orange, juiced and zest
finely pared

Method

1. Preheat the oven to 190°C (170°C fan) / 375F / gas 5 and line
   a 12-hole cupcake tin with paper cases.

2. Combine the flour, sugar, butter, eggs and orange zest in a
   bowl and whisk together for 2 minutes or until smooth.

3. Divide the mixture between the cases, then transfer the tin to
   the oven and bake for 18 minutes or until a skewer inserted in
   the centre of a cake comes out clean. Transfer the cakes to a
   wire rack and leave to cool completely.

4. Whip the crème fraiche with the icing sugar and 1 tbsp of
   orange juice until the mixture holds its shape, then spoon it
   into a piping bag fitted with a large star nozzle. Pipe a swirl on
   top of each cake and sprinkle with orange zest.

Smart tip

Using crème fraiche rather than double (heavy) cream adds a tangy element to these cakes.

Smart tip
To crumble the biscuits, put them in a sandwich bag then seal it up and crush with a rolling pin.

Cookie crumble cupcakes

Preparation time
40 minutes

Cooking time
18 minutes

Makes 12

Ingredients

110 g / 4 oz / 1 cup self-raising
   flour, sifted
110 g / 4 oz / ½ cup caster
   (superfine) sugar
110 g / 4 oz / ½ cup butter,
   softened
2 large eggs
2 tbsp unsweetened cocoa
   powder

To decorate:
300 ml / 10 ½ fl. oz / 1 ¼ cups
   double (heavy) cream
6 chocolate biscuits, crumbled

Method

1. Preheat the oven to 190°C (170°C fan) / 375F / gas 5 and line
   a 12-hole cupcake tin with paper cases.

2. Combine the flour, sugar, butter, eggs and cocoa powder in a
   bowl and whisk together for 2 minutes or until smooth.

3. Divide the mixture between the cases, then transfer the tin
   to the oven and bake for 18 minutes. Test with a wooden
   toothpick; if it comes out clean, the cakes are done. Transfer
   the cakes to a wire rack and leave to cool completely.

4. Whip the cream until it holds its shape, then spoon it into a
   piping bag fitted with a large star nozzle. Pipe a swirl of cream
   onto each cake and top with crumbled biscuit.

Mallow sprinkles cupcakes

Preparation time
35 minutes

Cooking time
18 minutes

Makes 12

Ingredients

110 g / 4 oz / 1 cup self-raising
flour, sifted
110 g / 4 oz / ½ cup caster
(superfine) sugar
110 g / 4 oz / ½ cup butter,
softened
2 large eggs
1 tsp vanilla extract

To decorate:
150 g / 5 ½ oz / 1 ½ cups
marshmallow fluff
4 tbsp sugar sprinkles

Method

1. Preheat the oven to 190°C (170°C fan) / 375F / gas 5 and line
a 12-hole cupcake tin with paper cases.

2. Combine the flour, sugar, butter, eggs and vanilla extract in a
bowl and whisk together for 2 minutes or until smooth.

3. Divide the mixture between the cake cases, then transfer the
tin to the oven and bake for 18 minutes. Test with a wooden
toothpick; if it comes out clean, the cakes are done. Transfer
the cakes to a wire rack and leave to cool completely.

4. Spread the cakes with marshmallow fluff. Tip the sugar
sprinkles into a small bowl, then dip in the tops of the cakes to
coat the marshmallow with sprinkles.

Smart tip

Marshmallow fluff can be purchased in jars from supermarkets and baking suppliers.

Smart tip

Look for chocolate chunks rather than smaller chocolate chips for the best presentation.

Vanilla chocolate cupcakes

Preparation time
45 minutes

Cooking time
18 minutes

Makes 12

Ingredients

110 g / 4 oz / 1 cup self-raising
flour, sifted

110 g / 4 oz / ½ cup caster
(superfine) sugar

110 g / 4 oz / ½ cup butter,
softened

2 large eggs

1 tsp vanilla extract

To decorate:

110 g / 4 oz / ½ cup butter,
softened

225 g / 8 oz / 2 cups icing
(confectioners') sugar, plus
extra for dusting

1 tsp vanilla extract

75 g / 2 ½ oz / ½ cup milk
chocolate chunks

Method

1. Preheat the oven to 190°C (170°C fan) / 375F / gas 5 and line
   a 12-hole cupcake tin with paper cases.

2. Combine the flour, sugar, butter, eggs and vanilla extract in a
   bowl and whisk together for 2 minutes or until smooth.

3. Divide the mixture between the cake cases, then transfer the
   tin to the oven and bake for 18 minutes. Test with a wooden
   toothpick; if it comes out clean, the cakes are done. Transfer
   the cakes to a wire rack and leave to cool completely.

4. To make the buttercream, beat the butter until smooth then
   beat in the icing sugar and vanilla extract.

5. Spoon the buttercream into a piping bag fitted with a large
   plain nozzle and pipe a swirl onto each cake, then top with
   chocolate chunks.

Candy flower cupcakes

Preparation time
40 minutes

Cooking time
18 minutes

Makes 12

Ingredients

110 g / 4 oz / 1 cup self-raising
   flour, sifted
110 g / 4 oz / ½ cup caster
   (superfine) sugar
110 g / 4 oz / ½ cup butter,
   softened
2 large eggs
½ tsp orange flower water

To decorate:
110 g / 4 oz / ½ cup butter,
   softened
225 g / 8 oz / 2 cups icing
   (confectioners') sugar, plus
   extra for dusting
1 tbsp rose water
a few drops of pink food dye
4 tbsp candy flowers

Method

1. Preheat the oven to 190°C (170°C fan) / 375F / gas 5 and line
   a 12-hole cupcake tin with paper cases.

2. Combine the flour, sugar, butter, eggs and orange flower
   water in a bowl and whisk together for 2 minutes or
   until smooth.

3. Divide the mixture between the cake cases then transfer the
   tin to the oven and bake for 18 minutes. Test with a wooden
   toothpick; if it comes out clean, the cakes are done. Transfer
   the cakes to a wire rack and leave to cool completely.

4. To make the buttercream, beat the butter until smooth then
   beat in the icing sugar, rose water and a few drops of pink
   food dye. Spread the icing over the cakes and sprinkle with
   candy flowers.

Smart tip
Rose water and
orange flower water
can be found in
the baking aisle of
supermarkets or
in Middle Eastern
shops.

Smart tip
Use a knife heated in
boiling water to spread
the ganache easily.

White chocolate ruby cupcakes

Preparation time
1 hour 20 minutes

Cooking time
10-15 minutes

Makes 12

Ingredients

110 g / 4 oz / 1 cup self-raising flour, sifted

110 g / 4 oz / ½ cup caster (superfine) sugar

110 g / 4 oz / ½ cup butter, softened

2 large eggs

1 tsp vanilla extract

75 g / 2 ½ oz / ½ cup white chocolate chips

To decorate:

200 g / 7 oz / 1 ⅓ cups white chocolate

200 ml / 7 fl. oz / ¾ cup double (heavy) cream

12 ruby sweets

Method

1. Preheat the oven to 190°C (170°C fan) / 375F / gas 5 and line a 12-hole cupcake tin with paper cases.

2. Combine the flour, sugar, butter, eggs and vanilla extract in a bowl and whisk together for 2 minutes or until smooth. Fold in the chocolate chips, then divide the mixture between the paper cases.

3. Transfer the tin to the oven and bake for 10–15 minutes. Test with a wooden toothpick; if it comes out clean, the cakes are done. Transfer the cakes to a wire rack and leave to cool completely.

4. Finely chop the chocolate and transfer it to a mixing bowl. Heat the cream until it starts to simmer, then pour it over the chocolate and leave to stand for 30 seconds. Slowly stir the chocolate and cream together until it forms a smooth ganache.

5. Leave the ganache to cool until it's thick enough to hold its shape, then spread it over the cakes and decorate each one with a ruby sweet.

Fondant sweet cupcakes

Preparation time
45 minutes

Cooking time
18 minutes

Makes 12

Ingredients

110 g / 4 oz / 1 cup self-raising
   flour, sifted
110 g / 4 oz / ½ cup caster
   (superfine) sugar
110 g / 4 oz / ½ cup butter,
   softened
2 large eggs
1 tsp vanilla extract

To decorate:
110 g / 4 oz / ½ cup butter,
   softened
225 g / 8 oz / 2 cups icing
   (confectioners') sugar, plus
   extra for dusting
1 tsp vanilla extract
150 g / 5 ½ oz / 1 cup
   fondant and jelly sweets

Method

1. Preheat the oven to 190°C (170°C fan) / 375F / gas 5 and line a 12-hole cupcake tin with paper cases.

2. Combine the flour, sugar, butter, eggs and vanilla extract in a bowl and whisk together for 2 minutes or until smooth.

3. Divide the mixture between the cake cases, then transfer the tin to the oven and bake for 18 minutes. Test with a wooden toothpick; if it comes out clean, the cakes are done. Transfer the cakes to a wire rack and leave to cool completely.

4. To make the buttercream, beat the butter until smooth then beat in the icing sugar and vanilla extract.

5. Spoon the buttercream into a piping bag fitted with a large star nozzle and pipe a swirl onto each cake, then top with the sweets.

Smart tip

Children love
helping to decorate
these cakes.

Smart tip

Buy the wafer flowers
online from cake
decorating specialists.

Flower fancy cupcakes

Preparation time
45 minutes

Cooking time
18 minutes

Makes 12

Ingredients

110 g / 4 oz / 1 cup self-raising
  flour, sifted
110 g / 4 oz / ½ cup caster
  (superfine) sugar
110 g / 4 oz / ½ cup butter,
  softened
2 large eggs
1 tsp rose water
½ tsp orange flower water

To decorate:
110 g / 4 oz / ½ cup butter,
  softened
225 g / 8 oz / 2 cups icing
  (confectioners') sugar, plus
  extra for dusting
½ tsp orange flower water
edible wafer flowers to
  decorate

Method

1. Preheat the oven to 190°C (170°C fan) / 375F / gas 5 and line
   a 12-hole cupcake tin with paper cases.

2. Combine the flour, sugar, butter, eggs and flower waters in a
   bowl and whisk together for 2 minutes or until smooth.

3. Divide the mixture between the cake cases then transfer the
   tin to the oven and bake for 18 minutes. Test with a wooden
   toothpick; if it comes out clean, the cakes are done. Transfer
   the cakes to a wire rack and leave to cool completely.

4. To make the buttercream, beat the butter until smooth then
   beat in the icing sugar and orange flower water.

5. Spoon the buttercream into a piping bag fitted with a large
   star nozzle and pipe a swirl onto each cake, then press the
   wafer flowers gently into the surface.

Strawberry shortcake cupcakes

Preparation time
45 minutes

Cooking time
18 minutes

Makes 12

Ingredients

110 g / 4 oz / 1 cup self-raising flour, sifted
110 g / 4 oz / ½ cup caster (superfine) sugar
110 g / 4 oz / ½ cup butter, softened
2 large eggs
1 tsp vanilla extract
3 tbsp freeze-dried strawberry pieces

To decorate:
300 ml / 10 ½ fl. oz / 1 ¼ cups double (heavy) cream
1 tbsp strawberry syrup
1 tbsp freeze-dried strawberry pieces
12 shortbread biscuits, halved

Method

1. Preheat the oven to 190°C (170°C fan) / 375F / gas 5 and line a 12-hole cupcake tin with paper cases.

2. Combine the flour, sugar, butter, eggs and vanilla extract in a bowl and whisk together for 2 minutes or until smooth, then fold in the strawberry pieces.

3. Divide the mixture between the cake cases, then transfer the tin to the oven and bake for 18 minutes. Test with a wooden toothpick; if it comes out clean, the cakes are done. Transfer the cakes to a wire rack and leave to cool completely.

4. Whip half of the cream with the syrup and strawberry pieces until it holds its shape, then spoon it into a piping bag fitted with a large star nozzle. Pipe a big swirl onto each cake.

5. Whip the rest of the cream and pipe a rosette onto the cakes, then top each one with half a shortbread biscuit.

6. Put the rest of the biscuit halves in a sandwich bag and crush with a rolling pin. Sprinkle the biscuit crumbs over the cakes to finish.

Smart tip

Serve the cakes within
1 hour to stop the
biscuits from
going soggy.

Smart tip

Piping on the buttercream gives a professional finish to these classic cupcakes.

Butterfly cupcakes

Preparation time
45 minutes

Cooking time
18 minutes

Makes 12

Ingredients

110 g / 4 oz / 1 cup self-raising
    flour, sifted
110 g / 4 oz / ½ cup caster
    (superfine) sugar
110 g / 4 oz / ½ cup butter,
    softened
2 large eggs
1 tsp vanilla extract

To decorate:
110 g / 4 oz / ½ cup butter,
    softened
225 g / 8 oz / 2 cups icing
    (confectioners') sugar, plus
    extra for dusting
1 tbsp milk
1 tsp vanilla extract
110 g / 4 oz / ½ cup
    strawberry jam (jelly)

Method

1. Preheat the oven to 190°C (170°C fan) / 375F / gas 5 and line a 12-hole cupcake tin with paper cases.

2. Combine the flour, sugar, butter, eggs and vanilla extract in a bowl and whisk together for 2 minutes or until smooth.

3. Divide the mixture between the cake cases, then transfer the tin to the oven and bake for 18 minutes. Test with a wooden toothpick; if it comes out clean, the cakes are done. Transfer the cakes to a wire rack and leave to cool completely.

4. To make the buttercream, beat the butter until smooth then beat in the icing sugar. Use a whisk to incorporate the milk and vanilla extract, then whisk for 2 minutes or until well whipped.

5. Spoon the icing into a piping bag fitted with a large star nozzle. Using a sharp knife, cut a shallow cone out of the centre of each cake and reserve.

6. Pipe a swirl of buttercream into the centre of each cake. Take the reserved cake pieces and cut each one in half to make the butterfly wings. Press the wings into the icing, then spoon on a line of jam to form the bodies. Dust lightly with icing sugar before serving.

Jelly bean cupcakes

Preparation time
45 minutes

Cooking time
18 minutes

Makes 12

Ingredients

110 g / 4 oz / 1 cup self-raising
   flour, sifted
110 g / 4 oz / ½ cup caster
   (superfine) sugar
110 g / 4 oz / ½ cup butter,
   softened
1 tsp vanilla extract
2 large eggs

To decorate:
200 g / 7 oz / 1 cup ready-to-
   roll fondant icing
3 tbsp royal icing
150 g / 5 ½ oz / 1 cup jelly
   beans

Method

1. Preheat the oven to 190°C (170°C fan) / 375F / gas 5 and line a 12-hole cupcake tin with paper cases.

2. Whisk the cake ingredients together until smooth, then divide between the paper cases.

3. Bake for 18 minutes or until a skewer inserted in the centre of a cake comes out clean. Leave to cool completely.

4. Roll out the fondant icing and use a plain round cookie cutter to cut out twelve circles. Wet the backs of the circles with a dab of water and smooth them onto the cakes.

5. Spoon the royal icing into a piping bag, then attach the jelly beans with small dots. Use the rest of the royal icing to pipe a pattern of dots on the cakes.

Smart tip

Try to use a mixture of beans on each cake for the best presentation.

Smart tip

For an adults-only treat, drizzle a tablespoon of amaretto liqueur over each cake when they come out of the oven.

Amaretti cupcakes

Preparation time
45 minutes

Cooking time
18 minutes

Makes 12

Ingredients

110 g / 4 oz / 1 cup self-raising
flour, sifted
110 g / 4 oz / ½ cup caster
(superfine) sugar
110 g / 4 oz / ½ cup butter,
softened
2 large eggs
1 tsp almond extract

To decorate:
110 g / 4 oz / ½ cup butter,
softened
225 g / 8 oz / 2 cups icing
(confectioners') sugar, plus
extra for dusting
1 tsp almond extract
12 amaretti biscuits, crumbled

Method

1. Preheat the oven to 190°C (170°C fan) / 375F / gas 5 and line
   a 12-hole cupcake tin with paper cases.

2. Combine the flour, sugar, butter, eggs and almond extract in a
   bowl and whisk together for 2 minutes or until smooth.

3. Divide the mixture between the cake cases, then transfer the
   tin to the oven and bake for 18 minutes. Test with a wooden
   toothpick; if it comes out clean, the cakes are done. Transfer
   the cakes to a wire rack and leave to cool completely.

4. To make the buttercream, beat the butter until smooth then
   beat in the icing sugar and almond extract.

5. Spoon the buttercream into a piping bag fitted with a large
   star nozzle and pipe a swirl onto each cake, then sprinkle with
   crushed amaretti biscuits.

Chocolate sweet cupcakes

Preparation time
35 minutes

Cooking time
18 minutes

Makes 12

Ingredients

110 g / 4 oz / 1 cup self-raising
   flour, sifted
110 g / 4 oz / ½ cup caster
   (superfine) sugar
110 g / 4 oz / ½ cup butter,
   softened
2 large eggs
1 lemon, zest finely grated

To decorate:

200 g / 7 oz / 2 cups icing
   (confectioners') sugar, plus
   extra for dusting
1 lemon, juiced
100 g / 3 ½ oz / ⅔ cup sugar-
   coated chocolate sweets
edible glitter for sprinkling

Method

1. Preheat the oven to 190°C (170°C fan) / 375F / gas 5 and line
   a 12-hole cupcake tin with paper cases.

2. Combine the flour, sugar, butter, eggs and lemon zest in a
   bowl and whisk together for 2 minutes or until smooth.

3. Divide the mixture between the cases, then transfer the tin to
   the oven and bake for 18 minutes or until a skewer inserted in
   the centre of a cake comes out clean. Transfer the cakes to a
   wire rack and leave to cool completely.

4. Sieve the icing sugar into a bowl and add just enough lemon
   juice to make a thick icing. Spoon the icing into a piping
   bag and snip off the end, then pipe zigzags across the top
   of the cakes.

5. Stud with the sugar-coated chocolate sweets and sprinkle
   with edible glitter.

Smart tip

Make a small hollow in the icing with your finger before topping with the cherry to keep it in place.

Bakewell cupcakes

Preparation time
40 minutes

Cooking time
18 minutes

Makes 12

Ingredients

110 g / 4 oz / 1 cup self-raising
   flour, sifted
110 g / 4 oz / ½ cup caster
   (superfine) sugar
110 g / 4 oz / ½ cup butter,
   softened
1 tsp almond extract
2 large eggs

To decorate:
200 g / 7 oz / 1 cup ready-to-
   roll fondant icing
12 glacé cherries

Method

1. Preheat the oven to 190°C (170°C fan) / 375F / gas 5 and line
   a 12-hole cupcake tin with paper cases.
2. Whisk the cake ingredients together until smooth, then divide
   between the paper cases.
3. Bake for 18 minutes or until a skewer inserted in the centre of
   a cake comes out clean. Leave to cool completely.
4. Roll out the fondant icing and use a plain round cookie cutter
   to cut out twelve circles. Wet the backs of the circles with a
   dab of water and smooth them onto the cakes, then top each
   one with a glacé cherry.

Frosted ginger cupcakes

Preparation time
45 minutes

Cooking time
18 minutes

Makes 12

Ingredients

110 g / 4 oz / 1 cup self-raising flour, sifted
110 g / 4 oz / ½ cup caster (superfine) sugar
110 g / 4 oz / ½ cup butter, softened
2 large eggs
1 tsp ground ginger

To decorate:
110 g / 4 oz / ½ cup butter, softened
225 g / 8 oz / 2 cups icing (confectioners') sugar, plus extra for dusting
1 tbsp ginger syrup
75 g / 2 ½ oz / ½ cup crystallised ginger, chopped

Method

1. Preheat the oven to 190°C (170°C fan) / 375F / gas 5 and line a 12-hole cupcake tin with paper cases.

2. Combine the flour, sugar, butter, eggs and ground ginger in a bowl and whisk together for 2 minutes or until smooth.

3. Divide the mixture between the cake cases, then transfer the tin to the oven and bake for 18 minutes. Test with a wooden toothpick; if it comes out clean, the cakes are done. Transfer the cakes to a wire rack and leave to cool completely.

4. To make the buttercream, beat the butter until smooth then beat in the icing sugar and ginger syrup.

5. Spoon the buttercream into a piping bag fitted with a large star nozzle and pipe a swirl onto each cake, then top with crystallised ginger.

Smart tip

Stem ginger can be used in place of the crystallised ginger.

Smart tip

Drizzling the piping bag with syrup gives a pretty rippled effect to the buttercream.

Blueberry swirl cupcakes

Preparation time
45 minutes

Cooking time
18 minutes

Makes 12

Ingredients

110 g / 4 oz / 1 cup self-raising
flour, sifted
110 g / 4 oz / ½ cup caster
(superfine) sugar
110 g / 4 oz / ½ cup butter,
softened
2 large eggs
1 tsp vanilla extract
75 g / 2 ½ oz / ½ cup
blueberries

To decorate:
110 g / 4 oz / ½ cup butter,
softened
225 g / 8 oz / 2 cups icing
(confectioners') sugar, plus
extra for dusting
4 tbsp blueberry syrup
12 blueberries

Method

1. Preheat the oven to 190°C (170°C fan) / 375F / gas 5 and line
a 12-hole cupcake tin with paper cases.

2. Combine the flour, sugar, butter, eggs and vanilla extract in a
bowl and whisk together for 2 minutes or until smooth, then
fold in the blueberries.

3. Divide the mixture between the cake cases, then transfer the
tin to the oven and bake for 18 minutes. Test with a wooden
toothpick; if it comes out clean, the cakes are done. Transfer
the cakes to a wire rack and leave to cool completely.

4. To make the buttercream, beat the butter until smooth then
beat in the icing sugar and half of the blueberry syrup.

5. Drizzle the rest of the syrup around the inside of a piping bag
fitted with a large star nozzle, then fill the bag with the
buttercream. Pipe the buttercream onto the cakes then top
each one with a blueberry.

Watermelon red velvet cupcakes

Preparation time
45 minutes

Cooking time
18 minutes

Makes 12

Ingredients

110 g / 4 oz / 1 cup self-raising flour, sifted
110 g / 4 oz / ½ cup caster (superfine) sugar
110 g / 4 oz / ½ cup butter, softened
2 large eggs
1 tbsp watermelon syrup
a few drops of red food dye
50 g / 1 ¾ oz / ¼ cup chocolate chunks

To decorate:

110 g / 4 oz / ½ cup butter, softened
225 g / 8 oz / 2 cups icing (confectioners') sugar, plus extra for dusting
1 tsp vanilla extract
green food dye
50 g / 1 ¾ oz / ¼ cup chocolate chunks

Method

1. Preheat the oven to 190°C (170°C fan) / 375F / gas 5 and line a 12-hole cupcake tin with paper cases.

2. Combine the flour, sugar, butter, eggs, watermelon syrup and food dye in a bowl and whisk together for 2 minutes or until smooth. Fold in the chocolate chunks.

3. Divide the mixture between the cake cases, then transfer the tin to the oven and bake for 18 minutes. Test with a wooden toothpick; if it comes out clean, the cakes are done. Transfer the cakes to a wire rack and leave to cool completely.

4. To make the buttercream, beat the butter until smooth then beat in the icing sugar, vanilla extract and a few drops of green food dye.

5. Spoon the buttercream into a piping bag fitted with a large star nozzle and pipe a swirl onto each cake, then decorate with chocolate chunks.

Smart tip

Watermelon syrup can be purchased from specialist coffee and cocktail suppliers.

Daisy cupcakes

Preparation time
45 minutes

Cooking time
18 minutes

Makes 12

Ingredients

110 g / 4 oz / 1 cup self-raising
    flour, sifted
110 g / 4 oz / ½ cup caster
    (superfine) sugar
110 g / 4 oz / ½ cup butter,
    softened
1 tsp vanilla extract
2 large eggs

To decorate:
200 g / 7 oz / 1 cup ready-to-
    roll blue fondant icing
3 tbsp royal icing
12 sugar paste daisies
24 edible wafer rose leaves

Method

1. Preheat the oven to 190°C (170°C fan) / 375F / gas 5 and line
   a 12-hole cupcake tin with paper cases.
2. Whisk the cake ingredients together until smooth, then divide
   between the paper cases.
3. Bake for 18 minutes or until a skewer inserted in the centre of
   a cake comes out clean. Leave to cool completely.
4. Roll out the fondant icing and use a plain round cookie cutter
   to cut out twelve circles. Wet the backs of the circles with a
   dab of water and smooth them onto the cakes.
5. Spoon the royal icing into a piping bag and pipe a ring of
   dots round the edge of each fondant circle, then attach the
   flowers and leaves with a little more royal icing.

Indulgent Cupcakes

Chocolate, nougat and caramel cupcakes

Preparation time
45 minutes

Cooking time
18 minutes

Makes 12

Ingredients

110 g / 4 oz / 1 cup self-raising
flour, sifted
2 tbsp cocoa powder
110 g / 4 oz / ½ cup caster
(superfine) sugar
110 g / 4 oz / ½ cup butter,
softened
2 large eggs
75 g / 1 ¾ oz / ⅔ cup
chocolate chunks

To decorate:
110 g / 4 oz / ½ cup butter,
softened
225 g / 8 oz / 2 cups icing
(confectioners') sugar, plus
extra for dusting
2 tbsp cocoa powder
4 tbsp dulce de leche
2 chocolate, nougat and
caramel bars, sliced

Method

1. Preheat the oven to 190°C (170°C fan) / 375F / gas 5 and line a 12-hole cupcake tin with paper cases.

2. Combine the flour, cocoa, sugar, butter and eggs in a bowl and whisk together for 2 minutes or until smooth, then fold in the chocolate chunks.

3. Divide the mixture between the cake cases, then transfer the tin to the oven and bake for 18 minutes. Test with a wooden toothpick; if it comes out clean, the cakes are done. Transfer the cakes to a wire rack and leave to cool completely.

4. To make the buttercream, beat the butter until smooth then beat in the icing sugar and cocoa powder. Spoon the mixture into a piping bag fitted with a large star nozzle and pipe a swirl on top of each cake.

5. Spoon a little dulce de leche onto the side of each one then top with sliced chocolate bar.

Smart tip

Folding in the chocolate chunks after whisking the cake mixture stops them from getting broken up.

Smart tip

Keep an eye on the meringue in the oven as it can burn easily.

Blackcurrant meringue cupcakes

Preparation time
55 minutes

Cooking time
23 minutes

Makes 12

Ingredients

110 g / 4 oz / 1 cup self-raising
  flour, sifted
110 g / 4 oz / ½ cup caster
  (superfine) sugar
110 g / 4 oz / ½ cup butter,
  softened
1 orange, zest finely grated
2 large eggs

To decorate:
4 large egg whites
110 g / 4 oz / ½ cup caster
  (superfine) sugar
100 ml / 3 ½ fl. oz / ½ cup
  blackcurrant jam (jelly)

Method

1. Preheat the oven to 190°C (170°C fan) / 375F / gas 5 and line a 12-hole cupcake tin with paper cases.

2. Whisk the cake ingredients together until smooth, then divide between the paper cases.

3. Bake for 18 minutes or until a skewer inserted in the centre of a cake comes out clean.

4. Whisk the egg whites until stiff, then gradually add the sugar and whisk until the mixture is thick and shiny. Spoon the meringue into a piping bag fitted with a large star nozzle.

5. Spread the blackcurrant jam over the cakes, then pipe small teardrops of meringue all over the surface.

6. Return the cakes to the oven and bake for a further 5 minutes or until the meringue is golden brown.

Chocolate rocher cupcakes

Preparation time
45 minutes

Cooking time
18 minutes

Makes 12

Ingredients

110 g / 4 oz / 1 cup self-raising
   flour, sifted
2 tbsp cocoa powder
110 g / 4 oz / ½ cup caster
   (superfine) sugar
110 g / 4 oz / ½ cup butter,
   softened
2 large eggs
75 g / 1 ¾ oz / ⅔ cup toasted
   hazelnuts (cobnuts),
   chopped

To decorate:

110 g / 4 oz / ½ cup butter,
   softened
225 g / 8 oz / 2 cups icing
   (confectioners') sugar,
   plus extra for dusting
2 tbsp cocoa powder
12 chocolate rochers

Method

1. Preheat the oven to 190°C (170°C fan) / 375F / gas 5 and line
   a 12-hole cupcake tin with paper cases.

2. Combine the flour, cocoa, sugar, butter and eggs in a bowl
   and whisk together for 2 minutes or until smooth, then fold
   in the hazelnuts.

3. Divide the mixture between the cake cases, then transfer the
   tin to the oven and bake for 18 minutes. Test with a wooden
   toothpick; if it comes out clean, the cakes are done. Transfer
   the cakes to a wire rack and leave to cool completely.

4. To make the buttercream, beat the butter until smooth
   then beat in the icing sugar and cocoa powder. Spoon the
   mixture into a piping bag fitted with a large star nozzle and
   pipe a rosette on top of each cake. Top each one with a
   chocolate rocher.

Smart tip

If the buttercream is a little stiff, add a few drops of milk to loosen it.

Smart tip

Use crunchy rather than smooth peanut butter for the best texture.

Cookie dough cupcakes

Preparation time
45 minutes

Cooking time
18 minutes

Makes 12

Ingredients

110 g / 4 oz / 1 cup self-raising flour, sifted

1 tbsp cocoa powder

110 g / 4 oz / ½ cup caster (superfine) sugar

110 g / 4 oz / ½ cup butter, softened

2 large eggs

2 tbsp crunchy peanut butter

3 tbsp chocolate chunks

To decorate:

110 g / 4 oz / ½ cup butter, softened

225 g / 8 oz / 2 cups icing (confectioners') sugar, plus extra for dusting

1 tsp vanilla extract

2 tbsp crunchy peanut butter

4 tbsp chocolate chunks

16 chocolate chip and peanut butter cookies

Method

1. Preheat the oven to 190°C (170°C fan) / 375F / gas 5 and line a 12-hole cupcake tin with paper cases.

2. Combine the flour, cocoa, sugar, butter, eggs and peanut butter in a bowl and whisk together for 2 minutes or until smooth, then fold in the chocolate chunks.

3. Divide the mixture between the cake cases, then transfer the tin to the oven and bake for 18 minutes. Test with a wooden toothpick; if it comes out clean, the cakes are done. Transfer the cakes to a wire rack and leave to cool completely.

4. To make the buttercream, beat the butter until smooth then beat in the icing sugar and vanilla extract. Spoon the mixture into a piping bag fitted with a large plain nozzle and pipe it onto the cakes.

5. Top each cake with a few chocolate chunks and a whole cookie, then crumble the remaining four cookies and sprinkle over the top.

Chocolate carrot cupcakes

Preparation time
1 hour

Cooking time
18 minutes

Makes 12

Ingredients

175 g / 6 oz / 1 cup soft light
   brown sugar
2 large eggs
150 ml / 5 fl. oz / ⅔ cup
   sunflower oil
175 g / 6 oz / 1 ¼ cups plain
   (all-purpose) flour
2 tsp baking powder
2 tbsp cocoa powder
200 g / 7 oz / 1 ⅔ cups carrots,
   peeled and coarsely grated

To decorate:
110 g / 4 oz / ½ cup butter,
   softened
225 g / 8 oz / 2 cups icing
   (confectioners') sugar, plus
   extra for dusting
2 tbsp cocoa powder
3 tbsp dark muscovado sugar
150 g / 5 ½ oz / ¾ cup ready-
   to-roll fondant icing
orange and green food dye

Method

1. Preheat the oven to 190°C (170°C fan) / 375F / gas 5 and
   line a 12-hole cupcake tin with paper cases.

2. Whisk the sugar, eggs and oil together for 3 minutes.
   Fold in the flour, baking powder and cocoa, followed by the
   grated carrots.

3. Divide the mixture between the paper cases, then transfer the
   tin to the oven and bake for 18 minutes. Test with a wooden
   toothpick; if it comes out clean, the cakes are done. Transfer
   the cakes to a wire rack and leave to cool completely.

4. To make the buttercream, beat the butter until smooth then
   beat in the icing sugar and cocoa powder. Spoon the mixture
   into a piping bag fitted with a large star nozzle and pipe a
   swirl on top of each cake. Sprinkle with muscovado sugar.

5. Add orange food dye to two thirds of the fondant and shape
   into the carrots. Add green dye to the rest and make the tops,
   attaching with a dab of water. Plant a fondant carrot into the
   top of each cake.

Smart tip

Rub the fondant carrots
with a little vegetable
oil to give them a shine.

Smart tip

These cupcakes also work well with blackberries and blackberry jam (jelly).

Raspberry mess cupcakes

Preparation time
45 minutes

Cooking time
10-15 minutes

Makes 12

Ingredients

110 g / 4 oz / 1 cup self-raising
    flour, sifted
110 g / 4 oz / ½ cup caster
    (superfine) sugar
110 g / 4 oz / ½ cup butter,
    softened
1 tsp vanilla extract
2 large eggs

To decorate:

4 tbsp raspberry jam (jelly)
400 ml / 14 fl. oz / 1 ⅔ cups
    double (heavy) cream
2 meringue nests, broken into
    pieces
36 raspberries
icing (confectioners') sugar for
    dusting

Method

1. Preheat the oven to 190°C (170°C fan) / 375F / gas 5 and line
   a 12-hole cupcake tin with paper cases.

2. Measure the cake ingredients into a bowl, then whisk
   together for 3 minutes or until smooth and light. Divide the
   mixture between the paper cases, then transfer the tin to the
   oven and bake for 10-15 minutes.

3. Test the cakes with a toothpick, if it comes out clean, the
   cakes are done. Transfer the cakes to a wire rack and leave to
   cool completely.

4. Cut a cone out of the centre of each cake and fill with jam,
   then replace the cone of cake.

5. Whip the cream until it holds its shape, then spoon a little
   onto each cake. Top each cake with a few pieces of meringue
   and 3 raspberries, then dust lightly with icing sugar.

Chocolate Turkish delight cupcakes

Preparation time
50 minutes

Cooking time
18 minutes

Makes 12

Ingredients

110 g / 4 oz / 1 cup self-raising flour, sifted
110 g / 4 oz / ½ cup caster (superfine) sugar
110 g / 4 oz / ½ cup butter, softened
2 large eggs
2 tbsp cocoa powder
1 tbsp rose water

To decorate:

110 g / 4 oz / ½ cup butter, softened
225 g / 8 oz / 2 cups icing (confectioners') sugar, plus extra for dusting
1 tbsp cocoa powder
½ tbsp rose water
pink food dye
150 g / 5 ½ oz / 1 cup Turkish delight, cubed
2 tbsp milk chocolate, grated

Method

1. Preheat the oven to 190°C (170°C fan) / 375F / gas 5 and line a 12-hole cupcake tin with paper cases.

2. Combine the flour, sugar, butter, eggs, cocoa powder and rose water in a bowl and whisk together for 2 minutes or until smooth.

3. Divide the mixture between the cake cases, then transfer the tin to the oven and bake for 18 minutes. Test with a wooden toothpick; if it comes out clean, the cakes are done. Transfer the cakes to a wire rack and leave to cool completely.

4. To make the buttercream, beat the butter until smooth then beat in the icing sugar. Divide the buttercream between two bowls and beat the cocoa powder into one and the rose water and a few drops of food dye into another.

5. Spoon the buttercreams into two separate piping bags fitted with star nozzles. Pipe a swirl of chocolate buttercream onto each cake and top with a swirl of rose buttercream.

6. Arrange the Turkish delight cubes on top of the cakes and sprinkle over a little grated chocolate.

Smart tip

Sieve the cocoa powder before adding it to the buttercream to incorporate it more easily.

Smart tip

These cupcakes are
a great twist on the
classic dessert.

Black forest cupcakes

Preparation time
1 hour

Cooking time
10-15 minutes

Makes 12

Ingredients

110 g / 4 oz / 1 cup self-raising
   flour, sifted
2 tbsp unsweetened cocoa
   powder
110 g / 4 oz / ½ cup caster
   (superfine) sugar
110 g / 4 oz / ½ cup butter,
   softened
2 large eggs
75 g / 2 ½ oz / ⅓ cup glacé
   cherries, chopped

To decorate:
4 tbsp black cherry jam (jelly)
200 ml / 7 fl. oz / ¾ cup
   double (heavy) cream
12 pitted black cherries in
   kirsch, drained
milk chocolate for grating

Method

1. Preheat the oven to 190°C (170°C fan) / 375F / gas 5 and line a 12-hole cupcake tin with paper cases.

2. Combine the flour, cocoa powder, sugar, butter and eggs in a bowl and whisk together for 2 minutes or until smooth. Fold in the cherries, then divide the mixture between the paper cases.

3. Transfer the tin to the oven and bake for 10-15 minutes. Test with a wooden toothpick; if it comes out clean, the cakes are done. Transfer the cakes to a wire rack and leave to cool completely.

4. Spread the top of each cake with cherry jam. Whip the cream until it holds its shape, then spoon it into a piping bag fitted with a large star nozzle. Pipe a ring around the edge of each cake.

5. Top each cake with a black cherry, then grate over a little milk chocolate.

Raspberry crown cupcakes

Preparation time
30 minutes

Cooking time
18 minutes

Makes 12

Ingredients

110 g / 4 oz / 1 cup self-raising
    flour, sifted
110 g / 4 oz / ½ cup caster
    (superfine) sugar
110 g / 4 oz / ½ cup butter,
    softened
2 large eggs
1 tsp almond extract

To decorate:
300 g / 10 ½ oz / 3 cups icing
    (confectioners') sugar, plus
    extra for dusting
1 lemon, juiced
225 g / 8 oz / 1 ½ cups
    raspberries

Method

1. Preheat the oven to 190°C (170°C fan) / 375F / gas 5 and line
   a 12-hole cupcake tin with paper cases.

2. Combine the flour, sugar, butter, eggs and almond extract in a
   bowl and whisk together for 2 minutes or until smooth.

3. Divide the mixture between the cases, then transfer the tin to
   the oven and bake for 18 minutes or until a skewer inserted in
   the centre of a cake comes out clean. Transfer the cakes to a
   wire rack and leave to cool completely.

4. Sieve the icing sugar into a bowl and add just enough lemon
   juice to make a thick, pourable icing.

5. Spoon a thick layer of icing onto the cakes and top with
   the raspberries.

Smart tip

Look out for heart-shaped plunger cutters which make light work of cutting the hearts.

Red velvet heart cupcakes

Preparation time
45 minutes

Cooking time
18 minutes

Makes 12

Ingredients

110 g / 4 oz / 1 cup self-raising
   flour, sifted
110 g / 4 oz / ½ cup caster
   (superfine) sugar
110 g / 4 oz / ½ cup butter,
   softened
2 large eggs
1 tsp vanilla extract
a few drops of red food dye

To decorate:

110 g / 4 oz / ½ cup cream
   cheese
55 g / 2 oz / ¼ cup butter,
   softened
110 g / 4 oz / 1 cup icing
   (confectioners') sugar
1 tbsp lemon juice
100 g / 3 ½ oz / ½ cup ready-
   to-roll red fondant icing

Method

1. Preheat the oven to 190°C (170°C fan) / 375F / gas 5 and
   line a 12-hole cupcake tin with paper cases.

2. Combine the flour, sugar, butter, eggs, vanilla extract
   and food dye in a bowl and whisk together for 2 minutes
   or until smooth.

3. Divide the mixture between the cake cases, then transfer
   the tin to the oven and bake for 18 minutes. Test with a
   wooden toothpick; if it comes out clean, the cakes are done.
   Transfer the cakes to a wire rack and leave to cool completely.

4. Beat the cream cheese and butter together until light and
   fluffy, then beat in the icing sugar a quarter at a time. Add
   the lemon juice, then whip the mixture for 2 minutes or
   until smooth and light. Spoon the icing into a piping bag
   fitted with a star nozzle and pipe a rosette onto each cake.

5. Roll out the red fondant and use a small heart-shaped cutter
   to cut out 24 hearts for the top of the cakes.

Neapolitan cupcakes

Preparation time
50 minutes

Cooking time
18 minutes

Makes 12

Ingredients

110 g / 4 oz / 1 cup self-raising
   flour, sifted
110 g / 4 oz / ½ cup caster
   (superfine) sugar
110 g / 4 oz / ½ cup butter,
   softened
2 large eggs
1 tsp vanilla extract

To decorate:
110 g / 4 oz / ½ cup butter,
   softened
225 g / 8 oz / 2 cups icing
   (confectioners') sugar, plus
   extra for dusting
1 tbsp cocoa powder
1 tbsp strawberry syrup
12 glacé cherries
sugar sprinkles

Method

1. Preheat the oven to 190°C (170°C fan) / 375F / gas 5 and line
   a 12-hole cupcake tin with paper cases.

2. Combine the flour, sugar, butter, eggs and vanilla extract in a
   bowl and whisk together for 2 minutes or until smooth.

3. Divide the mixture between the cake cases, then transfer the
   tin to the oven and bake for 18 minutes. Test with a wooden
   toothpick; if it comes out clean, the cakes are done. Transfer
   the cakes to a wire rack and leave to cool completely.

4. To make the buttercream, beat the butter until smooth then
   beat in the icing sugar. Divide the buttercream between
   three bowls and beat the cocoa powder into one and the
   strawberry syrup into another.

5. Spoon the buttercreams into three piping bags fitted with
   plain nozzles and pipe a swirl of each buttercream onto the
   cakes. Top the cakes with a glacé cherry and sugar sprinkles.

Smart tip

Be sure to use unsweetened cocoa powder rather than hot chocolate drink powder.

Smart tip

These cakes work well with any combination of berries that are in season.

Berries and cream cupcakes

Preparation time
45 minutes

Cooking time
10-15 minutes

Makes 12

Ingredients

110 g / 4 oz / 1 cup self-raising
  flour, sifted
110 g / 4 oz / ½ cup caster
  (superfine) sugar
110 g / 4 oz / ½ cup butter,
  softened
1 tsp vanilla extract
2 large eggs

To decorate:
400 ml / 14 fl. oz / 1 ⅔ cups
  double (heavy) cream
3 large strawberries, quartered
36 blueberries
36 raspberries
strawberry syrup for drizzling

Method

1. Preheat the oven to 190°C (170°C fan) / 375F / gas 5 and line
   a 12-hole cupcake tin with paper cases.

2. Measure the cake ingredients into a bowl, then whisk together
   for 3 minutes or until smooth and light. Divide the mixture
   between the paper cases, then transfer the tin to the oven and
   bake for 10–15 minutes.

3. Test the cakes with a toothpick, if it comes out clean, the
   cakes are done. Transfer the cakes to a wire rack and leave
   to cool completely.

4. Whip the cream until it holds its shape, then spoon it into a
   piping bag fitted with a large star nozzle and pipe a swirl on
   top of each cake.

5. Arrange the berries on top of the cakes and drizzle with a little
   strawberry syrup.

Nougat cupcakes

Preparation time
50 minutes

Cooking time
18 minutes

Makes 12

Ingredients

110 g / 4 oz / 1 cup self-raising flour, sifted
110 g / 4 oz / ½ cup caster (superfine) sugar
110 g / 4 oz / ½ cup butter, softened
2 large eggs
2 tbsp runny honey
1 tsp almond extract

To decorate:
110 g / 4 oz / ½ cup butter, softened
225 g / 8 oz / 2 cups icing (confectioners') sugar, plus extra for dusting
1 tbsp runny honey
½ tsp almond extract
a few drops of pink food dye
12 pieces of nougat

Method

1. Preheat the oven to 190°C (170°C fan) / 375F / gas 5 and line a 12-hole cupcake tin with paper cases.

2. Combine the flour, sugar, butter, eggs, honey and almond extract in a bowl and whisk together for 2 minutes or until smooth.

3. Divide the mixture between the cake cases, then transfer the tin to the oven and bake for 18 minutes. Test with a wooden toothpick; if it comes out clean, the cakes are done. Transfer the cakes to a wire rack and leave to cool completely.

4. To make the buttercream, beat the butter until smooth then beat in the icing sugar, honey and almond extract.

5. Spoon half of the buttercream into a piping bag, fitted with a large star nozzle and pipe a swirl on top of each cake.

6. Dye the rest of the buttercream pink, then pipe a smaller swirl on top of the white buttercream. Top each cake with a piece of nougat.

Smart tip

If you use nutty nougat to top the cakes, add 3 tbsp of chopped toasted almonds to the cake mixture.

Smart tip

Make sure the toffee bars aren't too cold when you chop them or the chocolate coating may fall off.

Toffee chocolate cupcakes

Preparation time
45 minutes

Cooking time
18 minutes

Makes 12

Ingredients

110 g / 4 oz / 1 cup self-raising flour, sifted

2 tbsp cocoa powder

110 g / 4 oz / ½ cup caster (superfine) sugar

110 g / 4 oz / ½ cup butter, softened

2 large eggs

50 g / 1 ¾ oz / ⅓ cup chocolate-coated toffee bars, chopped

To decorate:

110 g / 4 oz / ½ cup butter, softened

225 g / 8 oz / 2 cups icing (confectioners') sugar, plus extra for dusting

1 tbsp cocoa powder

1 tbsp dulce de leche

50 g / 1 ¾ oz / ⅓ cup chocolate-coated toffee bars, chopped

Method

1. Preheat the oven to 190°C (170°C fan) / 375F / gas 5 and line a 12-hole cupcake tin with paper cases.

2. Combine the flour, cocoa powder, sugar, butter and eggs in a bowl and whisk together for 2 minutes or until smooth, then fold in the toffee pieces.

3. Divide the mixture between the cake cases, then transfer the tin to the oven and bake for 18 minutes. Test with a wooden toothpick; if it comes out clean, the cakes are done. Transfer the cakes to a wire rack and leave to cool completely.

4. To make the buttercream, beat the butter until smooth then beat in the icing sugar, cocoa powder and dulce de leche. Spoon the mixture into a piping bag fitted with a large star nozzle and pipe a swirl on top of each cake. Arrange the chopped toffee bars on top.

Rocky road cupcakes

Preparation time
45 minutes

Cooking time
18 minutes

Makes 12

Ingredients

110 g / 4 oz / 1 cup self-raising
  flour, sifted
2 tbsp cocoa powder
110 g / 4 oz / ½ cup caster
  (superfine) sugar
110 g / 4 oz / ½ cup butter,
  softened
2 large eggs
3 tbsp raisins
3 tbsp honey-roasted peanuts

To decorate:

110 g / 4 oz / ½ cup butter,
  softened
225 g / 8 oz / 2 cups icing
  (confectioners') sugar, plus
  extra for dusting
2 tbsp cocoa powder
50 g / 1 ¾ oz / ¼ cup raisins
50 g / 1 ¾ oz / ¼ cup honey
  roasted peanuts
50 g / 1 ¾ oz / ¼ cup
  chocolate chunks
25 g / 1 oz / ½ cup mini
  marshmallows
4 tbsp milk chocolate, melted

Method

1. Preheat the oven to 190°C (170°C fan) / 375F / gas 5 and line a 12-hole cupcake tin with paper cases.

2. Combine the flour, cocoa, sugar, butter and eggs in a bowl and whisk together for 2 minutes or until smooth, then fold in the raisins and peanuts.

3. Divide the mixture between the cake cases, then transfer the tin to the oven and bake for 18 minutes. Test with a wooden toothpick; if it comes out clean, the cakes are done. Transfer the cakes to a wire rack and leave to cool completely.

4. To make the buttercream, beat the butter until smooth then beat in the icing sugar and cocoa powder. Spoon the mixture into a piping bag fitted with a large star nozzle and pipe a swirl on top of each cake.

5. Mix the raisins, peanuts, chocolate chunks and marshmallows together, then pack the mixture on top of the cakes.

6. Drizzle over the melted chocolate and leave to set before serving.

Smart tip

Use a small piping bag to drizzle the chocolate for the most professional finish.

Smart tip

Add the strawberries just before serving to keep them at their freshest.

Strawberry ripple cupcakes

Preparation time
40 minutes

Cooking time
10-15 minutes

Makes 12

Ingredients

110 g / 4 oz / 1 cup self-raising flour, sifted
110 g / 4 oz / ½ cup caster (superfine) sugar
110 g / 4 oz / ½ cup butter, softened
2 large eggs
1 tsp vanilla extract

To decorate:

110 g / 4 oz / ½ cup butter, softened
225 g / 8 oz / 2 cups icing (confectioners') sugar, plus extra for dusting
3 tbsp strawberry syrup
12 strawberries

Method

1. Preheat the oven to 190°C (170°C fan) / 375F / gas 5 and line a 12-hole cupcake tin with paper cases.

2. Combine the flour, sugar, butter, eggs and vanilla extract in a bowl and whisk together for 2 minutes or until smooth.

3. Divide the mixture between the cake cases, then transfer the tin to the oven and bake for 10–15 minutes. Test with a wooden toothpick; if it comes out clean, the cakes are done. Transfer the cakes to a wire rack and leave to cool completely.

4. To make the buttercream, beat the butter until smooth then beat in the icing sugar. Fold through the strawberry syrup to create a rippled effect, then spoon it onto the cakes.

5. Top each cake with a strawberry and a light dusting of icing sugar.

Chocolate banana cupcakes

Preparation time
45 minutes

Cooking time
18 minutes

Makes 12

Ingredients

110 g / 4 oz / 1 cup self-raising
   flour, sifted
2 tbsp cocoa powder
110 g / 4 oz / ½ cup caster
   (superfine) sugar
110 g / 4 oz / ½ cup butter,
   softened
2 large eggs
1 large banana, chopped

To decorate:
110 g / 4 oz / ½ cup butter,
   softened
225 g / 8 oz / 2 cups icing
   (confectioners') sugar, plus
   extra for dusting
2 tbsp cocoa powder
3 tbsp milk chocolate, grated
36 dried banana slices

Method

1. Preheat the oven to 190°C (170°C fan) / 375F / gas 5 and line
   a 12-hole cupcake tin with paper cases.

2. Combine the flour, cocoa, sugar, butter and eggs in a bowl
   and whisk together for 2 minutes or until smooth, then fold in
   the banana.

3. Divide the mixture between the cake cases, then transfer the
   tin to the oven and bake for 18 minutes. Test with a wooden
   toothpick; if it comes out clean, the cakes are done. Transfer
   the cakes to a wire rack and leave to cool completely.

4. To make the buttercream, beat the butter until smooth then
   beat in the icing sugar and cocoa powder. Spoon the mixture
   into a piping bag fitted with a large star nozzle and pipe a
   swirl on top of each cake.

5. Sprinkle the cakes with grated chocolate and top each one
   with three dried banana slices.

Smart tip
Remove most of the
food dye from the
brush onto kitchen
paper before
stippling.

Sugar apple cupcakes

Preparation time
1 hour

Cooking time
18 minutes

Makes 12

Ingredients

175 g / 6 oz / 1 cup soft light brown sugar

2 large eggs

150 ml / 5 fl. oz / ⅔ cup sunflower oil

175 g / 6 oz / 1 ¼ cups plain (all-purpose) flour

2 tsp baking powder

1 tsp ground cinnamon

200 g / 7 oz / 1 ⅔ cups dessert apples, peeled, cored and coarsely grated

To decorate:

110 g / 4 oz / ½ cup butter, softened

225 g / 8 oz / 2 cups icing (confectioners') sugar, plus extra for dusting

4 tbsp granulated sugar

150 g / 5 ½ oz / ¾ cup marzipan

green and red food dye

Method

1. Preheat the oven to 190°C (170°C fan) / 375F / gas 5 and line a 12-hole cupcake tin with paper cases.

2. Whisk the sugar, eggs and oil together for 3 minutes. Fold in the flour, baking powder and cinnamon, followed by the grated apple.

3. Divide the mixture between the paper cases, then transfer the tin to the oven and bake for 18 minutes. Test with a wooden toothpick; if it comes out clean, the cakes are done. Transfer the cakes to a wire rack and leave to cool completely.

4. To make the buttercream, beat the butter until smooth then beat in the icing sugar. Spread the icing over the cakes and sprinkle with granulated sugar.

5. Dye the marzipan green and shape into 12 apples with leaves. Use a small brush to stipple red food dye over part of each apple, then sit them on top of the cakes.

Rose cupcakes

Preparation time
45 minutes

Cooking time
18 minutes

Makes 12

Ingredients

110 g / 4 oz / 1 cup self-raising
  flour, sifted
110 g / 4 oz / ½ cup caster
  (superfine) sugar
110 g / 4 oz / ½ cup butter,
  softened
2 large eggs
1 tbsp rose water

To decorate:
110 g / 4 oz / ½ cup butter,
  softened
225 g / 8 oz / 2 cups icing
  (confectioners') sugar, plus
  extra for dusting
2 tsp rose water
a few drops of pink food dye

Method

1. Preheat the oven to 190°C (170°C fan) / 375F / gas 5 and line a 12-hole cupcake tin with paper cases.

2. Combine the flour, sugar, butter, eggs and rose water in a bowl and whisk together for 2 minutes or until smooth.

3. Divide the mixture between the cake cases, then transfer the tin to the oven and bake for 18 minutes. Test with a wooden toothpick; if it comes out clean, the cakes are done. Transfer the cakes to a wire rack and leave to cool completely.

4. To make the buttercream, beat the butter until smooth then beat in the icing sugar, rose water and a few drops of pink food dye.

5. Spoon half of the buttercream down one side of a piping bag fitted with a large star nozzle. Beat a little more food dye into the rest of the buttercream and spoon it into the other side of the bag. Pipe a spiral of buttercream onto each cake.

Smart tip

Start the buttercream spiral from the centre of the cake and work outwards to create a rose effect.

Smart tip

The cakes can be made a few days in advance, but top with the cream just before serving.

Mojito cupcakes

Preparation time
40 minutes

Cooking time
18 minutes

Makes 12

Ingredients

110 g / 4 oz / 1 cup self-raising
flour, sifted
110 g / 4 oz / ½ cup caster
(superfine) sugar
110 g / 4 oz / ½ cup butter,
softened
2 large eggs
1 tbsp mint leaves, very finely
chopped
2 limes, juiced and zest finely
grated
2 tbsp white rum

To decorate:
300 ml / 10 ½ fl. oz / 1 ¼ cups
double (heavy) cream
2 tbsp icing (confectioners')
sugar
1 tbsp white rum
1 tbsp lime juice
3 lime slices, quartered
12 sprigs of mint

Method

1. Preheat the oven to 190°C (170°C fan) / 375F / gas 5 and line
a 12-hole cupcake tin with paper cases.

2. Combine the flour, sugar, butter, eggs, mint and lime zest in a
bowl and whisk together for 2 minutes or until smooth.

3. Divide the mixture between the cases, then transfer the tin
to the oven and bake for 18 minutes. Test with a wooden
toothpick; if it comes out clean, the cakes are done. Mix the
lime juice with the rum and spoon it over the cakes, then leave
to cool completely.

4. Whip the cream with the icing sugar, rum and lime juice
until it holds its shape, then spoon it into a piping bag fitted
with a large star nozzle. Pipe a swirl on top of each cake and
decorate with lime and mint.

Caramel popcorn cupcakes

Preparation time
50 minutes

Cooking time
10-15 minutes

Makes 12

Ingredients

110 g / 4 oz / 1 cup self-raising
   flour, sifted
110 g / 4 oz / ½ cup caster
   (superfine) sugar
110 g / 4 oz / ½ cup butter,
   softened
2 large eggs
75 g / 2 ½ oz / ½ cup caramel
   pieces

To decorate:
100 g / 3 ½ oz / ½ cup butter,
   softened
200 g / 7 oz / 2 cups icing
   (confectioners') sugar
2 tbsp caramel syrup
200 g / 7 oz / 2 cups caramel-
   coated popcorn

Method

1. Preheat the oven to 190°C (170°C fan) / 375F / gas 5 and line a 12-hole cupcake tin with paper cases.

2. Combine the flour, sugar, butter, eggs and caramel pieces in a bowl and whisk together for 2 minutes or until smooth.

3. Divide the mixture between the cases, then transfer the tin to the oven and bake for 10-15 minutes. Test with a wooden toothpick; if it comes out clean, the cakes are done. Transfer the cakes to a wire rack and leave to cool completely.

4. Beat the butter until smooth, then gradually whisk in the icing sugar and caramel syrup. Spread the buttercream over the cakes and top with popcorn.

Smart tip

Caramel syrup is
available from specialist
coffee suppliers.

Smart tip

Decorate these cakes just before serving so the blackberry jam does not run into the cream.

Blackberry cream cupcakes

Preparation time
45 minutes

Cooking time
10-15 minutes

Makes 12

Ingredients

110 g / 4 oz / ⅔ cup self-
   raising flour, sifted
110 g / 4 oz / ½ cup caster
   (superfine) sugar
110 g / 4 oz / ½ cup butter,
   softened
1 tsp vanilla extract
2 large eggs

To decorate:
400 ml / 14 fl. oz / 1 ⅔ cups
   double (heavy) cream
6 tbsp blackberry jam (jelly)
icing (confectioners') sugar for
   dusting

Method

1. Preheat the oven to 190°C (170° fan) / 375F / gas 5 and line a
   12-hole cupcake tin with paper cases.

2. Measure the cake ingredients into a bowl then whisk together
   for 3 minutes or until smooth and light. Divide the mixture
   between the paper cases, then transfer the tin to the oven and
   bake for 10-15 minutes.

3. Test the cakes with a toothpick; if it comes out clean, the cakes
   are done. Transfer the cakes to a wire rack and leave to cool
   completely.

4. Whip the cream until it holds its shape, then spoon it into a
   piping bag fitted with a large star nozzle and pipe a ring of
   rosettes around the edge of each cake.

5. Fill the centres with blackberry jam, then dust them lightly
   with icing sugar.

Hazelnut chocolate cupcakes

Preparation time
40 minutes

Cooking time
10-15 minutes

Makes 12

Ingredients

110 g / 4 oz / 1 cup self-raising flour, sifted

2 tbsp unsweetened cocoa powder

110 g / 4 oz / ½ cup caster (superfine) sugar

110 g / 4 oz / ½ cup butter, softened

2 large eggs

75 g / 2 ½ oz / ½ cup roasted hazelnuts (cobnuts), chopped

To decorate:
400 ml / 14 fl. oz / 1 ½ cups hazelnut (cobnut) chocolate spread

Method

1. Preheat the oven to 190°C (170°C fan) / 375F / gas 5 and line a 12-hole cupcake tin with paper cases.

2. Combine the flour, cocoa powder, sugar, butter and eggs in a bowl and whisk together for 2 minutes or until smooth. Fold in the hazelnuts, then divide the mixture between the paper cases.

3. Transfer the tin to the oven and bake for 10-15 minutes. Test with a wooden toothpick; if it comes out clean, the cakes are done. Transfer the cakes to a wire rack and leave to cool completely.

4. Spoon the chocolate spread into a piping bag fitted with a large plain nozzle, then pipe a big swirl on top of each cake.

Smart tip

If you have any hazelnut (cobnut) pieces left over, these look nice scattered over the cakes.

Chocolate cherry treat cupcakes

Preparation time
45 minutes

Cooking time
18 minutes

Makes **12**

Ingredients

110 g / 4 oz / 1 cup self-raising flour, sifted

110 g / 4 oz / ½ cup caster (superfine) sugar

110 g / 4 oz / ½ cup butter, softened

2 large eggs

1 tsp vanilla extract

75 g / 2 ½ oz / ½ cup white chocolate chips

To decorate:

200 g / 7 oz / 1 ⅓ cups milk chocolate

200 ml / 7 fl. oz / ¾ cup double (heavy) cream

100 g / 3 ½ oz / ⅔ cup dark chocolate (minimum 60% cocoa solids)

12 fresh cherries

white chocolate vermicelli to sprinkle

Method

1. Preheat the oven to 190°C (170°C fan) / 375F / gas 5 and line a 12-hole cupcake tin with paper cases.

2. Combine the flour, sugar, butter, eggs and vanilla extract in a bowl and whisk together for 2 minutes or until smooth. Fold in the chocolate chips, then divide the mixture between the paper cases.

3. Transfer the tin to the oven and bake for 10–15 minutes. Test with a wooden toothpick; if it comes out clean, the cakes are done. Transfer the cakes to a wire rack and leave to cool completely.

4. Finely chop the milk chocolate and transfer it to a mixing bowl. Heat the cream until it starts to simmer, then pour it over the chocolate and leave to stand for 30 seconds. Slowly stir the chocolate and cream until it forms a smooth ganache.

5. Leave the ganache to cool until it's thick enough to hold its shape, then spoon it into a piping bag fitted with a large plain nozzle. Pipe a swirl of ganache onto each cake.

6. Melt the dark chocolate and drizzle it over the ganache, then top each one with a cherry and a sprinkle of white chocolate vermicelli.

Pineapple dream cupcakes

Preparation time
50 minutes

Cooking time
18 minutes

Makes 12

Ingredients

110 g / 4 oz / 1 cup self-raising
  flour, sifted
110 g / 4 oz / ½ cup caster
  (superfine) sugar
110 g / 4 oz / ½ cup butter,
  softened
2 large eggs
2 tbsp desiccated coconut
1 tsp coconut extract
75 g / 2 ½ oz / ⅓ cup glacé
  pineapple, chopped

To decorate:

110 g / 4 oz / ½ cup butter,
  softened
225 g / 8 oz / 2 cups icing
  (confectioners') sugar, plus
  extra for dusting
1 tsp coconut extract
1 tbsp desiccated coconut
300 g / 10 ½ oz / 1 ½ cups
  canned pineapple chunks,
  drained
12 glacé cherries

Method

1. Preheat the oven to 190°C (170°C fan) / 375F / gas 5 and line
   a 12-hole cupcake tin with paper cases.

2. Combine the flour, sugar, butter, eggs, desiccated coconut
   and coconut extract in a bowl and whisk together for
   2 minutes or until smooth, then fold in the glacé pineapple.

3. Divide the mixture between the cake cases, then transfer the
   tin to the oven and bake for 18 minutes. Test with a wooden
   toothpick; if it comes out clean, the cakes are done. Transfer
   the cakes to a wire rack and leave to cool completely.

4. To make the buttercream, beat the butter until smooth
   then beat in the icing sugar, coconut extract and coconut.
   Spoon the mixture into a piping bag and pipe a swirl on
   top of each cake.

5. Top the cakes with a ring of pineapple chunks and add a
   glacé cherry to the centre of each one.

Smart tip

Dry the pineapple chunks off on kitchen paper as any excess liquid can melt the sugar in the buttercream.

Smart tip

Keep the white chocolate quite chunky for the best texture.

Double chocolate cupcakes

Preparation time
45 minutes

Cooking time
18 minutes

Makes 12

Ingredients

110 g / 4 oz / 1 cup self-raising
  flour, sifted
2 tbsp cocoa powder
110 g / 4 oz / ½ cup caster
  (superfine) sugar
110 g / 4 oz / ½ cup butter,
  softened
2 large eggs
1 tsp vanilla extract
50 g / 1 ¾ oz / ⅓ cup white
  chocolate, chopped

To decorate:
110 g / 4 oz / ½ cup butter,
  softened
225 g / 8 oz / 2 cups icing
  (confectioners') sugar, plus
  extra for dusting
2 tbsp cocoa powder
1 chocolate flake bar

Method

1. Preheat the oven to 190°C (170°C fan) / 375F / gas 5 and line
   a 12-hole cupcake tin with paper cases.

2. Combine the flour, cocoa, sugar, butter, eggs and vanilla
   extract in a bowl and whisk together for 2 minutes or until
   smooth, then fold in the white chocolate.

3. Divide the mixture between the cake cases, then transfer the
   tin to the oven and bake for 18 minutes. Test with a wooden
   toothpick; if it comes out clean, the cakes are done. Transfer
   the cakes to a wire rack and leave to cool completely.

4. To make the buttercream, beat the butter until smooth then
   beat in the icing sugar and cocoa powder. Spoon the mixture
   into a piping bag fitted with a large star nozzle and pipe a
   swirl on top of each cake. Crumble the chocolate flake bar
   and sprinkle on top of the buttercream.

Occasion Cupcakes

Birthday balloon cupcakes

Preparation time
45 minutes

Cooking time
18 minutes

Makes 12

Ingredients

110 g / 4 oz / 1 cup self-raising
flour, sifted
110 g / 4 oz / ½ cup caster
(superfine) sugar
110 g / 4 oz / ½ cup butter,
softened
1 tsp vanilla extract
2 large eggs

To decorate:
350 g / 12 oz / 1 ¾ cups ready-
to-roll fondant icing
red and blue food dye
2 tbsp royal icing
edible glitter for sprinkling

Method

1. Preheat the oven to 190°C (170°C fan) / 375F / gas 5 and line
   a 12-hole cupcake tin with paper cases.

2. Whisk the cake ingredients together until smooth, then divide
   between the paper cases.

3. Bake for 18 minutes or until a skewer inserted in the centre of
   a cake comes out clean. Leave to cool completely.

4. Roll out half of the fondant icing and use a plain round cookie
   cutter to cut out 12 circles. Wet the backs of the circles with a
   dab of water and smooth them onto the cakes.

5. Divide the rest of the fondant in half and dye one piece blue
   and the other red. Model 12 balloons out of each piece and
   attach them to the cakes with a dab of water as before.

6. Spoon the royal icing into a piping bag fitted with a small
   plain nozzle and pipe on strings for the balloons. Finish the
   cakes with a sprinkle of glitter.

Smart tip

Buy the decorations from sugarcraft shops or online.

New baby cupcakes

Preparation time
45 minutes

Cooking time
18 minutes

Makes 12

Ingredients

110 g / 4 oz / 1 cup self-raising
  flour, sifted
110 g / 4 oz / ½ cup caster
  (superfine) sugar
110 g / 4 oz / ½ cup butter,
  softened
1 tsp vanilla extract
2 large eggs

To decorate:

350 g / 12 oz / 1 ¾ cups ready-
  to-roll fondant icing
blue food dye
2 tbsp royal icing
12 baby-themed sugar
  decorations

Method

1. Preheat the oven to 190°C (170°C fan) / 375F / gas 5 and line
   a 12-hole cupcake tin with paper cases.

2. Whisk the cake ingredients together until smooth, then divide
   between the paper cases.

3. Bake for 18 minutes or until a skewer inserted in the centre of
   a cake comes out clean. Leave to cool completely.

4. Roll out half of the fondant icing and use a plain round cookie
   cutter to cut out twelve circles. Wet the backs of the circles
   with a dab of water and smooth them onto the cakes.

5. Dye the rest of the fondant blue, then roll and cut out
   12 smaller circles, attaching as before.

6. Spoon the royal icing into a piping bag fitted with a small
   plain nozzle and pipe a ring of dots around the outside of the
   blue. Attach the sugar decorations with a blob of royal icing.

Wedding cupcakes

Preparation time
50 minutes

Cooking time
18 minutes

Makes 12

Ingredients

110 g / 4 oz / 1 cup self-raising
  flour, sifted
110 g / 4 oz / ½ cup caster
  (superfine) sugar
110 g / 4 oz / ½ cup butter,
  softened
1 tbsp rose water
2 large eggs

To decorate:
350 g / 12 oz / 1 ¾ cups ready-
  to-roll fondant icing
pink food dye
pink pearlised dusting powder
2 tbsp royal icing
12 white fondant roses
12 ribbons

Method

1. Preheat the oven to 190°C (170°C fan) / 375F / gas 5 and line
   a 12-hole cupcake tin with deep paper cases.

2. Whisk the cake ingredients together until smooth, then divide
   between the paper cases.

3. Bake for 18 minutes or until a skewer inserted in the centre of
   a cake comes out clean. Leave to cool completely.

4. Roll out a third of the fondant icing and use a plain round
   cookie cutter to cut out twelve circles. Wet the backs of the
   circles with a dab of water and smooth them onto the cakes.

5. Dye the rest of the fondant pink and roll it into 72 balls. Brush
   the balls with pearlised powder.

6. Attach six pink pearls to the top of each cake with a little royal
   icing, then add a rose to the centre of each one.

7. Tie a ribbon round the edge of each cake case to finish.

Smart tip

Secure the ribbons with a dab of glue so they don't fall down.

Smart tip

Use a small square cutter and a sharp knife to make the mortarboards.

Graduation iced cupcakes

Preparation time
1 hour 5 minutes

Cooking time
18 minutes

Makes 12

Ingredients

110 g / 4 oz / 1 cup self-raising
flour, sifted
110 g / 4 oz / ½ cup caster
(superfine) sugar
110 g / 4 oz / ½ cup butter,
softened
1 tsp vanilla extract
2 large eggs

To decorate:
350 g / 12 oz / 1 ¾ cups ready-
to-roll fondant icing
red, black and yellow food dye
edible glitter for sprinkling

Method

1. Preheat the oven to 190°C (170°C fan) / 375F / gas 5 and line
   a 12-hole cupcake tin with paper cases.

2. Whisk the cake ingredients together until smooth, then divide
   between the paper cases.

3. Bake for 18 minutes or until a skewer inserted in the centre of
   a cake comes out clean. Leave to cool completely.

4. Roll out half of the fondant icing and use a plain round cookie
   cutter to cut out twelve circles, reserving any off-cuts. Wet the
   backs of the circles with a dab of water and smooth them onto
   the cakes.

5. Dye two thirds of the remaining fondant red and roll it out.
   Use a smaller round cutter to cut out twelve circles and attach
   to the cakes as before.

6. Use the white fondant off-cuts to make the scrolls, then dye a
   small piece of fondant yellow to make the rings, adding a red
   seal to each.

7. Dye the rest of the icing black and shape it into the
   mortarboards, then finish them off with a sprinkle of glitter.

Fondant heart cupcakes

Preparation time
45 minutes

Cooking time
18 minutes

Makes 12

Ingredients

110 g / 4 oz / 1 cup self-raising
    flour, sifted
110 g / 4 oz / ½ cup caster
    (superfine) sugar
110 g / 4 oz / ½ cup butter,
    softened
1 tsp vanilla extract
2 large eggs

To decorate:
350 g / 12 oz / 1 ¾ cups ready-
    to-roll fondant icing
red food dye

Method

1. Preheat the oven to 190°C (170°C fan) / 375F / gas 5 and line
   a 12-hole cupcake tin with paper cases.

2. Whisk the cake ingredients together until smooth, then divide
   between the paper cases.

3. Bake for 18 minutes or until a skewer inserted in the centre of
   a cake comes out clean. Leave to cool completely.

4. Roll out half of the fondant icing and use a plain round cookie
   cutter to cut out six circles, reserving the off-cuts. Wet the
   backs of the circles with a dab of water and smooth them onto
   the cakes.

5. Dye the rest of the fondant red, then roll and cut out as before
   to top the other six cakes.

6. Use a heart-shaped cutter to cut out six white hearts and six
   red hearts and attach them to the contrasting cakes with a dab
   of water.

7. Roll any off-cuts into small balls and position them round the
   outside of the cakes.

Smart tip

Mark on the roof tiles, window and door details with a sharp knife, being careful not to cut all the way through.

New house cupcakes

Preparation time
1 hour

Cooking time
18 minutes

Makes 12

Ingredients

110 g / 4 oz / 1 cup self-raising flour, sifted

110 g / 4 oz / ½ cup caster (superfine) sugar

110 g / 4 oz / ½ cup butter, softened

1 tsp vanilla extract

2 large eggs

To decorate:

350 g / 12 oz / 1 ¾ cups ready-to-roll fondant icing

yellow, blue and red food dye

Method

1. Preheat the oven to 190°C (170°C fan) / 375F / gas 5 and line a 12-hole cupcake tin with paper cases.

2. Whisk the cake ingredients together until smooth, then divide between the paper cases.

3. Bake for 18 minutes or until a skewer inserted in the centre of a cake comes out clean. Leave to cool completely.

4. Roll out a third of the fondant icing and use a plain round cookie cutter to cut out twelve circles, reserving any off-cuts. Wet the backs of the circles with a dab of water and smooth them onto the cakes.

5. Dye a third of the remaining fondant yellow, then roll it out and cut out twelve squares for the walls.

6. Divide the remaining fondant in half and dye one piece red and the other blue. Roll out the blue fondant, then cut out and attach the roofs and chimneys with a dab of water.

7. Roll out the red fondant and make the doors and windows, then use a blossom plunger cutter to cut out the flowers and plunge them directly onto the cakes. Add a blue fondant door knob to each door.

Good luck cupcakes

Preparation time
1 hour 5 minutes

Cooking time
18 minutes

Makes 12

Ingredients

110 g / 4 oz / 1 cup self-raising
   flour, sifted
110 g / 4 oz / ½ cup caster
   (superfine) sugar
110 g / 4 oz / ½ cup butter,
   softened
2 tbsp Irish cream liqueur
2 large eggs

To decorate:
350 g / 12 oz / 1 ¾ cups ready-
   to-roll fondant icing
green and grey food dye
2 tbsp royal icing
edible silver metallic lustre
   dust
edible glitter for sprinkling

Method

1. Preheat the oven to 190°C (170°C fan) / 375F / gas 5 and line a 12-hole cupcake tin with paper cases.

2. Whisk the cake ingredients together until smooth, then divide between the paper cases.

3. Bake for 18 minutes or until a skewer inserted in the centre of a cake comes out clean. Leave to cool completely.

4. Roll out half of the fondant icing and use a plain round cookie cutter to cut out twelve circles, reserving any off-cuts. Wet the backs of the circles with a dab of water and smooth them onto the cakes.

5. Dye half of the remaining fondant green. Roll it out and use a heart-shaped cutter to make the shamrock leaves, pressing in the vein with a sharp knife. Use any off-cuts to make the stalks, then attach to the cakes with a dab of royal icing.

6. Dye the rest of the fondant grey, then roll it out and cut out the horseshoes. Use the end of a small round piping nozzle to mark on the nails, then brush them with silver lustre.

7. Attach the horseshoes to the cakes with a dab of royal icing, then use the rest to pipe a circle of dots round the edge of the white circles. Finish with a sprinkle of edible glitter.

Smart tip

Brush any excess lustre off the horseshoes with a dry brush so that it doesn't mark the cakes.

Smart tip

Try to keep the numbers as straight as possible when transferring them to the cakes so they don't get distorted.

21st birthday cupcakes

Preparation time
55 minutes

Cooking time
18 minutes

Makes 12

Ingredients

110 g / 4 oz / 1 cup self-raising
 flour, sifted
110 g / 4 oz / ½ cup caster
 (superfine) sugar
110 g / 4 oz / ½ cup butter,
 softened
1 tsp vanilla extract
2 large eggs

To decorate:

350 g / 12 oz / 1 ¾ cups ready-
 to-roll fondant icing
red and blue food dye
edible glitter for sprinkling

Method

1. Preheat the oven to 190°C (170°C fan) / 375F / gas 5 and line
 a 12-hole cupcake tin with paper cases.

2. Whisk the cake ingredients together until smooth, then divide
 between the paper cases.

3. Bake for 18 minutes or until a skewer inserted in the centre of
 a cake comes out clean. Leave to cool completely.

4. Roll out half of the fondant icing and use a plain round cookie
 cutter to cut out twelve circles. Wet the backs of the circles
 with a dab of water and smooth them onto the cakes.

5. Dye half of the remaining fondant red. Roll it out and use a
 smaller round cutter to make a circle for the centre of each
 cake, attaching as before.

6. Dye the rest of the fondant blue and use a "2" and a "1"
 shaped cutter to cut out the numbers, then wet the backs
 and smooth them onto the cakes. Finish with a sprinkle of
 edible glitter.

Spring chick cupcakes

Preparation time
55 minutes

Cooking time
18 minutes

Makes 12

Ingredients

110 g / 4 oz / ⅔ cup self-
   raising flour, sifted
110 g / 4 oz / ½ cup caster
   (superfine) sugar
110 g / 4 oz / ½ cup butter,
   softened
1 lemon, zest finely grated
2 large eggs

To decorate:
350 g / 12 oz / 1 ¾ cups ready-
   to-roll fondant icing
yellow and orange food dye
1 tbsp dark chocolate, melted
1 tbsp royal icing

Method

1. Preheat the oven to 190°C (170°C fan) / 375F / gas 5 and line a 12-hole cupcake tin with paper cases.

2. Whisk the cake ingredients together until smooth, then divide between the paper cases.

3. Bake for 18 minutes or until a skewer inserted in the centre of a cake comes out clean. Leave to cool completely.

4. Reserve a quarter of the fondant icing and dye the rest yellow. Roll it out and use a plain round cookie cutter to cut out twelve circles. Wet the backs of the circles with a dab of water and smooth them onto the cakes.

5. Dye any yellow off-cuts orange and use to make the beaks, feathers and feet. Roll out the reserved white fondant and cut out eggshell shapes for some of the cakes, then attach everything with a dab of water.

6. Spoon the chocolate and icing into separate piping bags and pipe on the eyes.

Smart tip

Use the same cookie cutter to cut the edges of the egg shells so they sit flush with the base circles.

Smart tip

Customise everyone's
cake to their favourite
brand of Champagne.

Iced Champagne cupcakes

Preparation time
1 hour 5 minutes

Cooking time
18 minutes

Makes 12

Ingredients

110 g / 4 oz / 1 cup self-raising
   flour, sifted
110 g / 4 oz / ½ cup caster
   (superfine) sugar
110 g / 4 oz / ½ cup butter,
   softened
2 tsp marc de Champagne
2 large eggs

To decorate:

350 g / 12 oz / 1 ¾ cups ready-
   to-roll fondant icing
green, black, yellow and red
   food dye
black food dye pen
edible glitter for sprinkling

Method

1. Preheat the oven to 190°C (170°C fan) / 375F / gas 5 and line a 12-hole cupcake tin with paper cases.

2. Whisk the cake ingredients together until smooth, then divide between the paper cases.

3. Bake for 18 minutes or until a skewer inserted in the centre of a cake comes out clean. Leave to cool completely.

4. Roll out half of the fondant icing and use a plain round cookie cutter to cut out twelve circles, reserving any off-cuts. Wet the backs of the circles with a dab of water and smooth them onto the cakes.

5. Dye half of the remaining fondant green and shape into 12 wine bottles, attaching as before.

6. Divide the rest of the fondant into three pieces and dye one black, one yellow and the other red. Use the black fondant to make the bottle foils, the yellow to make the seals and cork and use a small star plunger cutter to cut stars out of the red fondant.

7. Write the labels with a black food dye pen and finish with a sprinkle of edible glitter.

Christening cupcakes

Preparation time
1 hour 5 minutes

Cooking time
18 minutes

Makes 12

Ingredients

110 g / 4 oz / 1 cup self-raising
  flour, sifted
110 g / 4 oz / ½ cup caster
  (superfine) sugar
110 g / 4 oz / ½ cup butter,
  softened
1 tsp vanilla extract
2 large eggs

To decorate:
350 g / 12 oz / 1 ¾ cups ready-
  to-roll fondant icing
green, blue, yellow and pink
  food dye
black food dye pen

Method

1. Preheat the oven to 190°C (170°C fan) / 375F / gas 5 and line a 12-hole cupcake tin with paper cases.

2. Whisk the cake ingredients together until smooth, then divide between the paper cases.

3. Bake for 18 minutes or until a skewer inserted comes out clean. Leave to cool completely.

4. Roll out half of the fondant icing and use a plain round cookie cutter to cut out twelve circles, reserving any off-cuts. Wet the backs of the circles with a dab of water and smooth them onto the cakes. Use the off-cuts to make the pillows and shape the bodies.

5. Divide the rest of the fondant into four pieces and dye one pink, one yellow, one green and the other blue. Use the pink fondant to model the heads, marking on the eyes with a food dye pen.

6. Roll out the other pieces of fondant and cut out the blankets, adding the details with a cocktail stick.

7. Assemble the babies onto the cakes, attaching everything with a dab of water.

Smart tip

Using a cocktail stick to mark on eyebrows gives the faces more expression.

Smart tip

If you're making these cupcakes for a wedding, you could dye the fondant to match the bridesmaids' dresses.

Two-tier wedding cupcakes

Preparation time
1 hour 30 minutes

Cooking time
10-15 minutes

Makes 12

Ingredients

175 g / 6 oz / 1 ¼ cups
    self-raising flour, sifted
175 g / 6 oz / ¾ cup caster
    (superfine) sugar
175 g / 6 oz / ¾ cup butter,
    softened
3 large eggs
2 tsp vanilla extract

To decorate:

200 g / 7 oz / 2 cups icing
    (confectioners') sugar
200 g / 7 oz / ⅔ cup ready-to-
    roll fondant icing
pink and blue food dye

Method

1. Preheat the oven to 190°C (170°C fan) / 375F / gas 5 and line
   a standard 12-hole cupcake tin and a 12-hole mini cupcake tin
   with paper cases.

2. Combine the flour, sugar, butter, eggs and vanilla extract in
   a bowl and whisk together for 2 minutes or until smooth.
   Divide the mixture between the cases, then transfer the tins
   to the oven and bake for 10-15 minutes, removing the mini
   cupcakes after 8-10 minutes.

3. Test with a wooden toothpick. If it comes out clean, the
   cakes are done. Transfer the cakes to a wire rack and leave to
   cool completely.

4. Add a little water to the icing sugar, a few drops at a time,
   until it forms a smooth, spreadable icing. Spoon the icing onto
   the cakes and tap them lightly on the work surface to level it
   out into a smooth puddle. Sit a mini cupcake on top of each
   standard cupcake.

5. Dye a third of the fondant icing pink and a third blue, then roll
   out all three pieces. Use a small blossom plunger cutter to cut
   out little flowers and apply them around the base of the mini
   cupcakes. Add the centres with contrasting icing.

6. Reroll the icing offcuts and cut them into ribbons, then roll
   the ribbons up to make roses. Position 3 roses on top of
   each cake.

Tea party cupcakes

Preparation time
1 hour 15 minutes

Cooking time
18 minutes

Makes 12

Ingredients

110 g / 4 oz / 1 cup self-raising
   flour, sifted
110 g / 4 oz / ½ cup caster
   (superfine) sugar
110 g / 4 oz / ½ cup butter,
   softened
1 tsp vanilla extract
2 large eggs

To decorate:

450 g / 1 lb / 2 ¼ cups ready-
   to-roll fondant icing
red, blue, pink, brown and
   yellow food dye

Method

1. Preheat the oven to 190°C (170°C fan) / 375F / gas 5 and line
   a 12-hole cupcake tin with paper cases.

2. Whisk the cake ingredients together until smooth, then divide
   between the paper cases.

3. Bake for 18 minutes or until a skewer inserted in the centre of
   a cake comes out clean. Leave to cool completely.

4. Roll out a third of the fondant icing and use a plain round
   cookie cutter to cut out 12 circles. Wet the backs of the circles
   and smooth them onto the cakes.

5. Dye half of the rest of the fondant red and model into
   the teapots.

6. Divide the rest of the fondant into quarters and dye each
   piece a different shade. Shape the fondant into the teacups,
   plates and cakes, then assemble everything on top of the
   cakes with a dab of water.

Smart tip

Mark the details onto
the crockery with a
cocktail stick.

Spooky pumpkin cupcakes

Preparation time
1 hour

Cooking time
20 minutes

Makes 12

Ingredients

175 g / 6 oz / 1 cup soft
    brown sugar
2 large eggs
150 ml / 5 fl. oz / ¾ cup
    sunflower oil
175 g / 6 oz / 1 ¼ cups
    wholemeal flour
3 tsp baking powder
2 tsp ground cinnamon
1 orange, zest finely grated
200 g / 7 oz / 1 cup pumpkin
    or butternut squash, peeled
    and coarsely grated

To decorate:

450 g / 1 lb / 2 ¼ cups ready-
    to-roll fondant icing
black, orange and green
    food dye
edible glitter for sprinkling

Method

1. Preheat the oven to 190°C (170°C fan) / 375F / gas 5 and line
   a 12-hole cupcake tin with paper cases.

2. Whisk the sugar, eggs and oil together for 3 minutes, then
   fold in the flour, baking powder and cinnamon, followed by
   the orange zest and pumpkin.

3. Divide the mixture between the paper cases and bake for
   20 minutes or until a skewer inserted in the centre of a cake
   comes out clean. Leave to cool completely.

4. Dye a third of the fondant black, then roll it out and cut out
   12 circles, reserving any off-cuts. Wet the backs of the circles
   with a dab of water and smooth them onto the cakes.

5. Dye three quarters of the remaining fondant orange and
   shape it into the pumpkins, adding the details with the blade
   of a small knife.

6. Dye the final piece of fondant green and make it into the
   stalks, then add eyes and noses made from the black off-cuts.

7. Finish the cakes with a sprinkle of glitter.

Bride and groom cupcakes

Preparation time
1 hour 5 minutes

Cooking time
18 minutes

Makes 12

Ingredients

110 g / 4 oz / 1 cup self-raising
  flour, sifted
110 g / 4 oz / ½ cup caster
  (superfine) sugar
110 g / 4 oz / ½ cup butter,
  softened
1 tsp vanilla extract
2 large eggs

To decorate:
350 g / 12 oz / 1 ¾ cups ready-
  to-roll fondant icing
black, pink and yellow food
  dye
3 tbsp royal icing
6 edible silver balls

Method

1. Preheat the oven to 190°C (170°C fan) / 375F / gas 5 and line
   a 12-hole cupcake tin with paper cases.

2. Whisk the cake ingredients together until smooth, then divide
   between the paper cases.

3. Bake for 18 minutes or until a skewer inserted in the centre of
   a cake comes out clean. Leave to cool completely.

4. Dye a third of the fondant icing pink, then roll it out and cut
   out six circles with a plain round cookie cutter. Wet the backs
   of the circles with a dab of water, then smooth them onto six
   of the cakes.

5. Dye half of the rest of the fondant black, then roll out and cut
   out six circles for the other cakes. Make the off-cuts into the
   lapels, buttons and bow ties.

6. Roll out the remaining white icing and make the wedding
   dresses and shirts, then dye the white off-cuts yellow and
   make a rose for each lapel.

7. Spoon the royal icing into a piping bag fitted with a small
   plain nozzle and pipe detailing onto the dress and a string of
   pearls for each bride. Use the royal icing to attach a silver ball
   in the centre of each bow tie.

Smart tip
Attach the fondant flames to the cakes with a little buttercream.

Bonfire cupcakes

Preparation time
1 hour

Cooking time
18 minutes

Makes 12

Ingredients

110 g / 4 oz / 1 cup self-raising
    flour, sifted
110 g / 4 oz / ½ cup caster
    (superfine) sugar
110 g / 4 oz / ½ cup butter,
    softened
2 large eggs
1 tsp vanilla extract

To decorate:

110 g / 4 oz / ½ cup butter,
    softened
225 g / 8 oz / 2 cups icing
    (confectioners') sugar, plus
    extra for dusting
1 tsp vanilla extract
orange, red and yellow food
    dye
12 chocolate flake bars
150 g / 5 ½ oz / ¾ cup ready-
    to-roll fondant icing

Method

1. Preheat the oven to 190°C (170°C fan) / 375F / gas 5 and line
   a 12-hole cupcake tin with paper cases.

2. Combine the flour, sugar, butter, eggs and vanilla extract in a
   bowl and whisk together for 2 minutes or until smooth.

3. Divide the mixture between the cake cases then transfer the
   tin to the oven and bake for 18 minutes. Test with a wooden
   toothpick; if it comes out clean, the cakes are done. Transfer
   the cakes to a wire rack and leave to cool completely.

4. To make the buttercream, beat the butter until smooth then
   beat in the icing sugar, vanilla extract and a few drops of
   orange food dye. Spoon the buttercream into a piping bag
   fitted with a large star nozzle.

5. Break the chocolate flakes into smaller 'logs' and assemble
   into a bonfire on top of each cake, interspersed with piped
   buttercream flames.

6. Divide the fondant icing into three pieces and dye one red,
   one yellow and one orange, then marble together to make
   the flames for the top of the bonfires.

Fondant snowman cupcakes

Preparation time
1 hour 10 minutes

Cooking time
18 minutes

Makes 12

Ingredients

110 g / 4 oz / 1 cup self-raising
    flour, sifted
110 g / 4 oz / ½ cup caster
    (superfine) sugar
110 g / 4 oz / ½ cup butter,
    softened
1 tsp vanilla extract
2 large eggs

To decorate:
450 g / 1 lb / 2 ¼ cups
    ready-to-roll fondant icing
red, green, brown, orange,
    black and blue food dye
2 tbsp royal icing
edible glitter for sprinkling

Method

1. Preheat the oven to 190°C (170°C fan) / 375F / gas 5 and line
   a 12-hole cupcake tin with paper cases.

2. Whisk the cake ingredients together until smooth, then divide
   between the paper cases.

3. Bake for 18 minutes or until a skewer inserted in the centre
   of a cake comes out clean. Leave to cool completely.

4. Set aside half of the fondant icing to make the snowmen.
   Dye a third of the rest of the fondant red and a third
   green, then roll them out. Use a plain round cookie cutter
   to cut out six circles from each, reserving any off-cuts. Wet
   the backs of the circles with a dab of water and smooth them
   onto the cakes.

5. Divide the final third of the fondant into four pieces and
   dye one piece blue, one black, one orange and one brown.
   Set aside.

6. Shape the reserved white fondant into 12 snowmen and
   attach them to the cakes with a dab of water. Decorate the
   snowmen with hats, scarves, noses, eyes and buttons using
   the different fondants, attaching the details as before with a
   dab of water.

7. Spoon the royal icing into a piping bag fitted with a small
   plain nozzle and pipe the snowflakes falling behind them.
   Finish the cakes with a sprinkle of edible glitter.

Smart tip

Using fondant icing and
a round cutter gives a
professional finish to
the top of the cakes.

Iced winter cupcakes

Preparation time
45 minutes

Cooking time
18 minutes

Makes 12

Ingredients

110 g / 4 oz / 1 cup self-raising
   flour, sifted
110 g / 4 oz / ½ cup caster
   (superfine) sugar
110 g / 4 oz / ½ cup butter,
   softened
1 tsp vanilla extract
2 large eggs

To decorate:

225 g / 8 oz / 1 cup ready-to-
   roll fondant icing
200 g / 7 oz / 2 cups icing
   (confectioners') sugar
edible silver balls to decorate

Method

1. Preheat the oven to 190°C (170°C fan) / 375F / gas 5 and line a 12-hole cupcake tin with paper cases.

2. Whisk the cake ingredients together until smooth, then divide between the paper cases.

3. Bake for 18 minutes or until a skewer inserted in the centre of a cake comes out clean. Leave to cool completely.

4. Roll out the fondant icing and use a plain round cookie cutter to cut out 12 circles. Wet the backs of the circles with a dab of water and smooth them onto the cakes.

5. Sieve the icing sugar into a bowl, then add just enough cold water to form a thick, pipeable icing. Spoon the icing into a piping bag fitted with a small plain nozzle.

6. Pipe a Christmas tree on top of each cake and add a few snowballs round the edge of the fondant. Press a silver ball onto the end of each branch of the Christmas tree, then leave the icing to set.

Holly fondant cupcakes

Preparation time
45 minutes

Cooking time
18 minutes

Makes 12

Ingredients

110 g / 4 oz / 1 cup self-raising
   flour, sifted
110 g / 4 oz / ½ cup caster
   (superfine) sugar
110 g / 4 oz / ½ cup butter,
   softened
1 tsp vanilla extract
2 large eggs

To decorate:
350 g / 12 oz / 1 ¾ cups ready-
   to-roll fondant icing
red and green food dye

Method

1. Preheat the oven to 190°C (170°C fan) / 375F / gas 5 and line a 12-hole cupcake tin with paper cases.

2. Whisk the cake ingredients together until smooth, then divide between the paper cases.

3. Bake for 18 minutes or until a skewer inserted in the centre of a cake comes out clean. Leave to cool completely.

4. Roll out two thirds of the fondant icing and use a plain round cookie cutter to cut out twelve circles. Wet the backs of the circles with a dab of water and smooth them onto the cakes.

5. Divide the rest of the fondant in half and dye one piece green and the other red. Roll out the green fondant and use a holly leaf cutter to cut out 24 holly leaves. Mark on the veins with a sharp knife, then wet the backs and smooth two onto each cake.

6. Roll the red icing into 36 balls, then wet the backs and stick them onto the cakes to form the berries.

Smart tip

Press hard with the holly leaf cutter to get a crisp edge to the leaves.

Novelty Cupcakes

Vanilla bird cupcakes

Preparation time
45 minutes

Cooking time
18 minutes

Makes 12

Ingredients

110 g / 4 oz / 1 cup self-raising
  flour, sifted
110 g / 4 oz / ½ cup caster
  (superfine) sugar
110 g / 4 oz / ½ cup butter,
  softened
2 large eggs
1 vanilla pod, seeds only

To decorate:
110 g / 4 oz / ½ cup butter,
  softened
225 g / 8 oz / 2 cups icing
  (confectioners') sugar, plus
  extra for dusting
1 tsp vanilla extract
12 paper bird cocktail sticks

Method

1. Preheat the oven to 190°C (170°C fan) / 375F / gas 5 and line
   a 12-hole cupcake tin with paper cases.

2. Combine the flour, sugar, butter, eggs and vanilla seeds in a
   bowl and whisk together for 2 minutes or until smooth.

3. Divide the mixture between the cake cases, then transfer the
   tin to the oven and bake for 18 minutes. Test with a wooden
   toothpick; if it comes out clean, the cakes are done. Transfer
   the cakes to a wire rack and leave to cool completely.

4. To make the buttercream, beat the butter until smooth then
   beat in the icing sugar and vanilla extract.

5. Spoon the buttercream into a piping bag fitted with a large
   star nozzle and pipe a swirl onto each cake, then top with the
   paper birds.

Smart tip

Soft light brown sugar creates the illusion of slightly damp sand perfectly.

Beach sandals cupcakes

Preparation time
1 hour

Cooking time
18 minutes

Makes 12

Ingredients

110 g / 4 oz / 1 cup self-raising
  flour, sifted
110 g / 4 oz / ½ cup caster
  (superfine) sugar
110 g / 4 oz / ½ cup butter,
  softened
2 large eggs
2 tbsp desiccated coconut
1 tsp coconut extract

To decorate:

110 g / 4 oz / ½ cup butter,
  softened
225 g / 8 oz / 2 cups icing
  (confectioners') sugar, plus
  extra for dusting
1 tsp coconut extract
3 tbsp soft light brown sugar
150 g / 5 ½ oz / ¾ cup ready-
  to-roll fondant icing
blue and red food dye
12 paper drinks umbrellas

Method

1. Preheat the oven to 190°C (170°C fan) / 375F / gas 5 and line
   a 12-hole cupcake tin with paper cases.

2. Combine the flour, sugar, butter, eggs, desiccated coconut
   and coconut extract in a bowl and whisk together for
   2 minutes or until smooth.

3. Divide the mixture between the cake cases then transfer the
   tin to the oven and bake for 18 minutes. Test with a wooden
   toothpick; if it comes out clean, the cakes are done. Transfer
   the cakes to a wire rack and leave to cool completely.

4. To make the buttercream, beat the butter until smooth
   then beat in the icing sugar and coconut extract. Spread the
   buttercream onto the cakes and sprinkle with brown sugar.

5. Dye three quarters of the fondant blue and shape into the
   soles of the sandals. Reserve a small piece of white fondant,
   then turn the rest red and make into the straps, attaching with
   a dab of water.

6. Roll out the reserved white fondant and use a small star
   plunger cutter to cut out the stars, attaching as before.
   Insert a drinks umbrella into each cake to finish.

Puppy dog cupcakes

Preparation time
1 hour 15 minutes

Cooking time
18 minutes

Makes 12

Ingredients

110 g / 4 oz / 1 cup self-raising
   flour, sifted
110 g / 4 oz / ½ cup caster
   (superfine) sugar
110 g / 4 oz / ½ cup butter,
   softened
1 tsp vanilla extract
2 large eggs

To decorate:
450 g / 1 lb / 2 ¼ cups ready-
   to-roll fondant icing
blue, brown, black and red
   food dye
black food dye pen
2 tbsp royal icing
edible glitter for sprinkling

Method

1. Preheat the oven to 190°C (170°C fan) / 375F / gas 5 and line a 12-hole cupcake tin with paper cases.

2. Whisk the cake ingredients together until smooth, then divide between the paper cases.

3. Bake for 18 minutes or until a skewer inserted in the centre of a cake comes out clean. Leave to cool completely.

4. Dye a quarter of the fondant green and roll it out, then use a plain round cookie cutter to cut out 12 circles. Wet the backs and smooth them onto the cakes.

5. Reserve a small piece of fondant, then dye the rest brown and model three quarters of it into 12 dogs. Dye the rest of the brown fondant a darker shade, then use it to make the ears, muzzles, rumps and tails.

6. Make the eyes from white fondant then add the pupils with a food dye pen. Dye a small piece of fondant black for the noses then turn the rest red and shape it into 12 balls.

7. Assemble the dogs on top of the cakes with a little royal icing, then use the rest to pipe dots round the outside of the blue circles. Finish with a sprinkle of edible glitter.

Smart tip
You can also buy
ready-dyed fondant
from cake decorating
suppliers.

Fried egg cupcakes

Preparation time
40 minutes

Cooking time
18 minutes

Makes 12

Ingredients

110 g / 4 oz / 1 cup self-raising
   flour, sifted
110 g / 4 oz / ½ cup caster
   (superfine) sugar
110 g / 4 oz / ½ cup butter,
   softened
2 tbsp cocoa powder
1 tsp vanilla extract
2 large eggs

To decorate:
350 g / 12 oz / 1 ¾ cups ready-
   to-roll fondant icing
yellow food dye

Method

1. Preheat the oven to 190°C (170°C fan) / 375F / gas 5 and line
   a 12-hole cupcake tin with foil cases.
2. Whisk the cake ingredients together until smooth, then divide
   between the foil cases.
3. Bake for 18 minutes or until a skewer inserted in the centre of
   a cake comes out clean. Leave to cool completely.
4. Roll out half of the fondant icing and use a flower-shaped
   cutter to cut out 12 shapes. Wet the backs of the flowers with
   a dab of water and smooth them onto the cakes to form the
   egg whites.
5. Dye the rest of the fondant icing yellow, then divide into
   12 pieces and roll into balls. Flatten the balls slightly, then
   attach the 'yolks' to the 'whites' with a dab of water.

Intergalactic cupcakes

Preparation time
55 minutes

Cooking time
18 minutes

Makes 12

Ingredients

110 g / 4 oz / 1 cup self-raising
   flour, sifted
110 g / 4 oz / ½ cup caster
   (superfine) sugar
110 g / 4 oz / ½ cup butter,
   softened
2 tbsp cocoa powder
2 large eggs

To decorate:
350 g / 12 oz / 1 ¾ cups ready-
   to-roll fondant icing
red, yellow and blue food dye
1 tbsp royal icing
edible silver balls
edible glitter for sprinkling

Method

1. Preheat the oven to 190°C (170°C fan) / 375F / gas 5 and line a 12-hole cupcake tin with paper cases.

2. Whisk the cake ingredients together until smooth, then divide between the paper cases.

3. Bake for 18 minutes or until a skewer inserted in the centre of a cake comes out clean. Leave to cool completely.

4. Dye two thirds of the fondant icing blue and use a plain round cookie cutter to cut out 12 circles. Wet the backs of the circles with a dab of water and smooth them onto the cakes.

5. Dye two thirds of the remaining fondant red, then shape it to make the planets, attaching with a little royal icing.

6. Dye the rest of the fondant yellow then roll it out and use star-shaped plunger cutters to cut out two different sizes of stars.

7. Attach the stars and silver balls with royal icing, then finish with a sprinkle of edible glitter.

Smart tip

Press down hard with the cutters to get a clean edge to the fondant shapes.

Funky caterpillar cupcakes

Preparation time
1 hour 5 minutes

Cooking time
18 minutes

Makes 12

Ingredients

110 g / 4 oz / 1 cup self-raising
  flour, sifted
110 g / 4 oz / ½ cup caster
  (superfine) sugar
110 g / 4 oz / ½ cup butter,
  softened
1 tsp vanilla extract
2 large eggs

To decorate:

350 g / 12 oz / 1 ¾ cups ready-
  to-roll fondant icing
green, blue, yellow and red
  food dye
black food dye pen

Method

1. Preheat the oven to 190°C (170°C fan) / 375F / gas 5 and line
   a 12-hole cupcake tin with paper cases.

2. Whisk the cake ingredients together until smooth, then divide
   between the paper cases.

3. Bake for 18 minutes or until a skewer inserted in the centre of
   a cake comes out clean. Leave to cool completely.

4. Roll out a third of the fondant icing and use a plain round
   cookie cutter to cut out 12 circles, reserving any off-cuts.
   Wet the backs of the circles with a dab of water and smooth
   them onto the cakes.

5. Dye a third of the remaining fondant green, then roll it out
   and use a flower-shaped cutter to cut out 12 shapes, attaching
   as before.

6. Divide the remaining fondant in half and dye one piece
   red and the other blue. Roll the fondant into balls to form
   12 caterpillars.

7. Use the white off-cuts to make the flowers and eyes, then
   turn any leftovers yellow to make the flower centres. Use a
   food dye pen to mark the pupils onto the eyes.

Goldfish bowl cupcakes

Preparation time
1 hour 10 minutes

Cooking time
18 minutes

Makes 12

Ingredients

110 g / 4 oz / ⅔ cup self-
  raising flour, sifted
110 g / 4 oz / ½ cup caster
  (superfine) sugar
110 g / 4 oz / ½ cup butter,
  softened
1 tsp vanilla extract
2 large eggs

To decorate:
450 g / 1 lb / 2 ¼ cups ready-
  to-roll fondant icing
green, blue, orange and grey
  food dye
4 tbsp royal icing

Method

1. Preheat the oven to 190°C (170°C fan) / 375F / gas 5 and line a 12-hole cupcake tin with paper cases.

2. Whisk the cake ingredients together until smooth, then divide between the paper cases.

3. Bake for 18 minutes or until a skewer inserted in the centre of a cake comes out clean. Leave to cool completely.

4. Dye a third of the fondant green, then roll it out and cut out 12 circles with a plain round cookie cutter. Wet the backs and smooth them onto the cakes.

5. Dye two thirds of the rest of the fondant blue and model it into twelve goldfish bowls.

6. Divide the off-cuts of the fondant in half and dye one piece grey and the other orange. Shape the orange fondant into the goldfish and attach to the bowls with a dab of water. Use the grey fondant to make pebbles for the bottom of the bowls.

7. Dye half of the royal icing green and pipe on some water plants. Use the rest of the white royal icing to pipe on the bubbles and add dots to the outside of the green circles.

Smart tip

Use a cocktail stick dipped in black food dye to mark the eyes or use a food dye pen.

Smart tip

Mark on whiskers and claws with a sharp craft knife.

Cat and mouse cupcakes

Preparation time
1 hour 10 minutes

Cooking time
18 minutes

Makes 12

Ingredients

110 g / 4 oz / 1 cup self-raising
   flour, sifted
110 g / 4 oz / ½ cup caster
   (superfine) sugar
110 g / 4 oz / ½ cup butter,
   softened
1 tsp vanilla extract
2 large eggs

To decorate:
450 g / 1 lb / 2 ¼ cups ready-
   to-roll fondant icing
yellow, grey and pink food dye
black food dye pen
2 tbsp royal icing

Method

1. Preheat the oven to 190°C (170°C fan) / 375F / gas 5 and line
   a 12-hole cupcake tin with paper cases.

2. Whisk the cake ingredients together until smooth, then divide
   between the paper cases.

3. Bake for 18 minutes or until a skewer inserted in the centre of
   a cake comes out clean. Leave to cool completely.

4. Dye a third of the fondant yellow, then roll it out and cut out
   12 circles with a plain round cookie cutter. Wet the backs and
   smooth them onto the cakes.

5. Dye two thirds of the rest of the fondant grey and model it
   into twelve cats. Save a small piece of white fondant for the
   eyes, then dye the rest pink and make the mice and the ears
   and noses for the cats. Add the whites of the eyes, then draw
   on the pupils with a black food dye pen.

6. Attach the figures to the top of the cakes with a little royal
   icing, then use the rest to pipe a ring of dots round the
   outside of the yellow circles.

Bumblebee cupcakes

Preparation time
1 hour 5 minutes

Cooking time
18 minutes

Makes 12

Ingredients

110 g / 4 oz / 1 cup self-raising
flour, sifted

110 g / 4 oz / ½ cup caster
(superfine) sugar

110 g / 4 oz / ½ cup butter,
softened

1 tbsp runny honey

2 large eggs

To decorate:

350 g / 12 oz / 1 ¾ cups ready-
to-roll fondant icing

green, purple, black and
yellow food dye

black food dye pen

edible glitter for sprinkling

Method

1. Preheat the oven to 190°C (170°C fan) / 375F / gas 5 and line
   a 12-hole cupcake tin with paper cases.

2. Whisk the cake ingredients together until smooth, then divide
   between the paper cases.

3. Bake for 18 minutes or until a skewer inserted in the centre of
   a cake comes out clean. Leave to cool completely.

4. Roll out half of the fondant icing and use a plain round cookie
   cutter to cut out 12 circles, reserving any off-cuts. Wet the
   backs of the circles with a dab of water and smooth them onto
   the cakes.

5. Dye a quarter of the remaining fondant green, then roll it out
   and cut out 12 flower shapes, attaching as before.

6. Dye another quarter purple and use a small blossom cutter
   to make the flowers, adding a small ball of leftover white
   fondant to the centre of each.

7. Dye another quarter black to make the bees' bodies and
   turn the final quarter yellow and make the stripes. Use white
   fondant off-cuts to make the wings and eyes, then draw on
   the pupils and mouths with a black food dye pen. Finish with
   a sprinkle of edible glitter.

Smart tip

Make the bee
decorations in advance
and store in an airtight
container.

Smart tip

Mark the details onto the beach creatures with a cocktail stick.

Beach creature cupcakes

Preparation time
1 hour 15 minutes

Cooking time
18 minutes

Makes 12

Ingredients

110 g / 4 oz / 1 cup self-raising
  flour, sifted
110 g / 4 oz / ½ cup caster
  (superfine) sugar
110 g / 4 oz / ½ cup butter,
  softened
1 tsp vanilla extract
2 large eggs

To decorate:
450 g / 1 lb / 2 ¼ cups ready-
  to-roll fondant icing
blue, orange, yellow, brown
  and green food dye
black food dye pen
1 tbsp soft light brown sugar

Method

1. Preheat the oven to 190°C (170°C fan) / 375F / gas 5 and line a 12-hole cupcake tin with paper cases.

2. Whisk the cake ingredients together until smooth, then divide between the paper cases.

3. Bake for 18 minutes or until a skewer inserted in the centre of a cake comes out clean. Leave to cool completely.

4. Dye half of the fondant icing blue then roll it out and cut out 12 circles with a plain round cookie cutter. Wet the backs of the circles with a dab of water and smooth them onto the cakes.

5. Save a small piece of fondant for the eyes, then divide the rest of the fondant into quarters and dye one orange, one yellow, one brown and one green. Model the fishes from the orange fondant and turn any off-cuts into coral.

6. Model the starfishes from the yellow fondant and turn the off-cuts into coral as before. Make the turtles from brown and green fondant then use any green off-cuts to make the seaweed. Use the reserved white fondant to make the eyes and bubbles, then draw on pupils with the food dye pen.

7. Attach the beach creatures to the top of the cakes with a dab of water and sprinkle on a little brown sugar sand.

Squirrel cupcakes

Preparation time
1 hour 5 minutes

Cooking time
18 minutes

Makes 10

Ingredients

110 g / 4 oz / 1 cup self-raising
   flour, sifted
110 g / 4 oz / ½ cup caster
   (superfine) sugar
110 g / 4 oz / ½ cup butter,
   softened
2 tbsp cocoa powder
2 tbsp chestnut spread
2 large eggs

To decorate:
150 g / 5 ½ oz / ⅔ cup
   chestnut spread
350 g / 12 oz / 1 ¾ cups ready-
   to-roll fondant icing
brown and black food dye

Method

1. Preheat the oven to 190°C (170°C fan) / 375F / gas 5 and line a 12-hole cupcake tin with paper cases.

2. Whisk the cake ingredients together until smooth, then divide between the paper cases.

3. Bake for 18 minutes or until a skewer inserted in the centre of a cake comes out clean. Leave to cool completely.

4. Spread ten of the cakes with chestnut spread, then crumble the remaining two cakes over the top of the others.

5. Dye three quarters of the fondant brown and model into the squirrels, then use some of the remaining white fondant to make the eyes, tummy and tail tuft.

6. Dye any off-cuts dark grey and use to make the pupils and noses, then sit the squirrels on top of the cakes.

Smart tip

Make the cars a day in advance and store them in a sealed container in the fridge.

Racing car cupcakes

Preparation time
1 hour 30 minutes

Cooking time
10-15 minutes

Makes 12

Ingredients

110 g / 4 oz / 1 cup self-raising
flour, sifted
110 g / 4 oz / ½ cup caster
(superfine) sugar
110 g / 4 oz / ½ cup butter,
softened
2 large eggs
1 tsp vanilla extract

To decorate:
150 g / 5 ½ oz / 1 ½ cups icing
(confectioners') sugar
200 g / 7 oz / ¾ cup ready-to-
roll fondant icing
black, green, blue and yellow
food dye

Method

1. Preheat the oven to 190°C (170°C fan) / 375F / gas 5 and line
a 12-hole cupcake tin with paper cases.

2. Combine the flour, sugar, butter, eggs and vanilla extract in a
bowl and whisk together for 2 minutes or until smooth. Divide
the mixture between the cases, then transfer the tin to the
oven and bake for 10-15 minutes.

3. Test with a wooden toothpick; if it comes out clean, the
cakes are done. Transfer the cakes to a wire rack and leave
to cool completely.

4. Add a little water to the icing sugar, a few drops at a time,
until it forms a smooth, spreadable icing. Reserve a little
icing for the decoration, then spoon the rest onto the cakes
and tap them lightly on the work surface to level it out into
a smooth puddle.

5. Dye a quarter of the fondant icing grey, then roll it out and cut
out 12 circles. Lay the circles on top of the cakes and add a
little more black food dye to the off-cuts before shaping them
into the wheels and helmet visors.

6. Make 12 helmets from a small piece of the white fondant,
then divide the rest into 3 pieces and dye them green,
blue and yellow. Model them into the cars, then assemble
everything on top of the cakes.

Ladybird cupcakes

Preparation time
1 hour 5 minutes

Cooking time
18 minutes

Makes 12

Ingredients

110 g / 4 oz / 1 cup self-raising flour, sifted
110 g / 4 oz / ½ cup caster (superfine) sugar
110 g / 4 oz / ½ cup butter, softened
2 large eggs
1 tsp vanilla extract

To decorate:
110 g / 4 oz / ½ cup butter, softened
225 g / 8 oz / 2 cups icing (confectioners') sugar, plus extra for dusting
1 tsp vanilla extract
green food dye
150 g / 5 ½ oz / ¾ cup ready-to-roll red fondant icing
75 g / 2 ½ oz / ⅓ cup ready-to-roll black fondant icing
1 tbsp white ready-to-roll fondant icing
black food dye pen
24 edible wafer leaves
florist's wire

Method

1. Preheat the oven to 190°C (170°C fan) / 375F / gas 5 and line a 12-hole cupcake tin with paper cases.

2. Combine the flour, sugar, butter, eggs and vanilla extract in a bowl and whisk together for 2 minutes or until smooth.

3. Divide the mixture between the cake cases, then transfer the tin to the oven and bake for 18 minutes. Test with a wooden toothpick; if it comes out clean, the cakes are done. Transfer the cakes to a wire rack and leave to cool completely.

4. To make the buttercream, beat the butter until smooth then beat in the icing sugar, vanilla extract and a few drops of green food dye. Spoon the buttercream into a piping bag fitted with a large star nozzle and pipe a swirl onto each cake.

5. Shape the red fondant into the ladybird bodies and use the black fondant to make the heads. Roll the white fondant into small balls and flatten them onto the heads to make the eyes, then draw on all the details with a black food dye pen.

6. Sit the ladybirds on top of the buttercream and add a couple of wafer leaves to each. Make the antennae out of florist's wire and insert into the heads.

Smart tip

The chestnut spread follows the woodland theme of these cakes but can be replaced with chocolate spread.

Owl cupcakes

Preparation time
1 hour 5 minutes

Cooking time
18 minutes

Makes 10

Ingredients

110 g / 4 oz / ⅔ cup self-
  raising flour, sifted
110 g / 4 oz / ½ cup caster
  (superfine) sugar
110 g / 4 oz / ½ cup butter,
  softened
2 tbsp cocoa powder
2 tbsp chestnut spread
2 large eggs

To decorate:
150 g / 5 ½ oz / ⅔ cup
  chestnut spread
350 g / 12 oz / 1 ¾ cups ready-
  to-roll fondant icing
brown, black, yellow and
  green food dye

Method

1. Preheat the oven to 190°C (170°C fan) / 375F / gas 5 and line a 12-hole cupcake tin with paper cases.

2. Whisk the cake ingredients together until smooth, then divide between the paper cases.

3. Bake for 18 minutes or until a skewer inserted in the centre of a cake comes out clean. Leave to cool completely.

4. Spread ten of the cakes with chestnut spread, then crumble the remaining two cakes into a bowl and reserve.

5. Dye two thirds of the fondant brown and model into the owls, using any off-cuts to make a log for each owl to sit on.

6. Use some of the remaining white fondant to make the eyes. Dye a small off-cut dark grey and use to make the pupils and dye another yellow for the beaks.

7. Dye the rest of the fondant two different shades of green and shape into leaves then assemble everything on top of the cakes. Finish with a sprinkle of cake crumbs.

Fondant butterfly cupcakes

Preparation time
overnight

Cooking time
18 minutes

Makes 12

Ingredients

110 g / 4 oz / 1 cup self-raising
   flour, sifted
110 g / 4 oz / ½ cup caster
   (superfine) sugar
110 g / 4 oz / ½ cup butter,
   softened
1 tsp vanilla extract
2 large eggs

To decorate:
350 g / 12 oz / 1 ¾ cups ready-
   to-roll fondant icing
purple food dye
4 tbsp royal icing
pearlised dusting powder

Method

1. Preheat the oven to 190°C (170°C fan) / 375F / gas 5 and line
   a 12-hole cupcake tin with paper cases.

2. Whisk the cake ingredients together until smooth, then divide
   between the paper cases.

3. Bake for 18 minutes or until a skewer inserted in the centre of
   a cake comes out clean. Leave to cool completely.

4. Dye half of the fondant purple and roll it out, then use a plain
   round cookie cutter to cut out twelve circles. Wet the backs of
   the circles with a dab of water and smooth them onto
   the cakes.

5. Roll out the rest of the fondant fairly thick, then use a butterfly
   plunger cutter to cut out and emboss the butterflies. Fold a
   piece of card into an 'M' shape and lay the butterflies in a line
   down the centre to harden overnight.

6. The next day, brush the butterflies with pearlised dusting
   powder, then attach to the cakes with a blob of royal icing.
   Use the rest of the royal icing to decorate the cakes with
   small dots.

Smart tip

Make the butterflies in advance and store in an airtight container.

Smart tip

If you have trouble forcing the fondant through a sieve, try chilling it for 30 minutes, then use a fine cheese grater.

Sporty ball cupcakes

Preparation time
50 minutes

Cooking time
18 minutes

Makes 12

Ingredients

110 g / 4 oz / 1 cup self-raising
  flour, sifted
110 g / 4 oz / ½ cup caster
  (superfine) sugar
110 g / 4 oz / ½ cup butter,
  softened
1 tsp vanilla extract
2 large eggs

To decorate:
350 g / 12 oz / 1 ¾ cups green
  ready-to-roll fondant icing
12 edible football wafers

Method

1. Preheat the oven to 190°C (170°C fan) / 375F / gas 5 and line
   a 12-hole cupcake tin with paper cases.

2. Whisk the cake ingredients together until smooth, then divide
   between the paper cases.

3. Bake for 18 minutes or until a skewer inserted in the centre of
   a cake comes out clean. Leave to cool completely.

4. Roll out the green fondant icing and cut out twelve circles with
   a plain round cookie cutter. Wet the backs of the circles with a
   dab of water, then smooth them onto the cakes.

5. Push the off-cuts through a sieve to make the grass, then
   brush a little water onto the fondant circles to fix it in place.
   Top each cake with an edible football wafer.

Sheep cupcakes

Preparation time
1 hour

Cooking time
10-15 minutes

Makes 12

Ingredients

Ingredients:
110 g / 4 oz / ⅔ cup
    self-raising flour, sifted
110 g / 4 oz / ½ cup caster
    (superfine) sugar
110 g / 4 oz / ½ cup butter,
    softened
2 large eggs
1 tsp vanilla extract

To decorate:
110 g / 4 oz / ½ cup butter,
    softened
225 g / 8 oz / 2 ¼ cups icing
    (confectioners') sugar
2 tbsp milk
1 tsp vanilla extract
75 g / 2 ½ oz / 1 ¼ cups mini
    marshmallows
100 g / 3 ½ oz / ½ cup ready-
    to-roll fondant icing
black food dye
12 sugar flowers

Method

1. Preheat the oven to 190°C (170°C fan) / 375F / gas 5 and line a 12-hole cupcake tin with paper cases.

2. Combine the flour, sugar, butter, eggs and vanilla extract in a bowl and whisk together for 2 minutes or until smooth.

3. Divide the mixture between the cake cases then transfer the tin to the oven and bake for 10-15 minutes. Test with a wooden toothpick; if it comes out clean, the cakes are done. Transfer the cakes to a wire rack and leave to cool completely.

4. To make the buttercream, beat the butter until smooth, then beat in the icing sugar. Use a whisk to incorporate the milk and vanilla extract, then whisk for 2 minutes or until well whipped.

5. Spread the buttercream onto the cakes and top with the marshmallows.

6. Reserve a small piece of white fondant icing for the eyes and dye the rest grey. Shape into the sheep heads, ears and pupils, adding the whites of the eyes with the reserved fondant. Position the heads on top of the cakes and add a sugar flower to each one.

Smart tip

You can find mini
marshmallows in the
baking aisle of most
supermarkets.

Smart tip

You can find ready-made fondant animals in specialised food stores.

Sleepy slow-worm cupcakes

Preparation time
1 hour 20 minutes

Cooking time
10-15 minutes

Makes 12

Ingredients

110 g / 4 oz / ⅔ cup self-
  raising flour, sifted
110 g / 4 oz / ½ cup caster
  (superfine) sugar
110 g / 4 oz / ½ cup butter,
  softened
2 large eggs
1 tsp vanilla extract

To decorate:
400 g / 14 oz ready to roll
  fondant icing
blue, pink and yellow food dye
black food dye pen

Method

1. Preheat the oven to 190°C (170° fan) / 375F / gas 5 and line a 12-hole cupcake tin with paper cases.

2. Combine the flour, sugar, butter, eggs and vanilla extract in a bowl and whisk together for 2 minutes or until smooth. Divide the mixture between the cases, then transfer the tin to the oven and bake for 10–15 minutes.

3. Test with a wooden toothpick; if it comes out clean, the cakes are done. Transfer the cakes to a wire rack and leave to cool completely.

4. Roll out a third of the fondant icing, then cut out 12 circles a little smaller than the diameter of the cakes. Wet the backs of the circles with a dab of water, then smooth them onto the cakes.

5. Dye a quarter of the remaining fondant yellow, then roll it out and cut out 12 large flowers. Lay them on top of the cakes. Save a small piece of white fondant for the eyes, then split the rest into 2 pieces and dye them blue and pink. Model some of the fondant into the slow-worms and make the eyes with the white fondant, adding the pupils with the black food dye pen.

6. Cut out the flowers with blossom-shaped plunger cutters and apply them directly onto the cakes.

Index